HEAVENLY
RESCUES
& ANSWERED PRAYERS

ANDREA JO RODGERS

HARVEST HOUSE PUBLISHERS
EUGENE, OREGON

Published in association with the Steve Laube Agency, LLC, 24 W. Camelback Rd., A-635, Phoenix, Arizona 85013.

Cover design by Bryce Williamson

Cover images © imagedepotpro, Caiaimage/Robert Daly / Getty Images

Interior design by KUHN Design Group

For bulk, special sales, or ministry purchases, please call 1-800-547-8979.
Email: Customerservice@hhpbooks.com

Names and minor details have been changed in the real-life stories shared in this book to protect the privacy of the individuals mentioned.

Heavenly Rescues and Answered Prayers
Copyright © 2024 by Andrea Jo Rodgers
Published by Harvest House Publishers
Eugene, Oregon 97408
www.harvesthousepublishers.com

ISBN 978-0-7369-9001-1 (pbk)
ISBN 978-0-7369-9002-8 (eBook)

Library of Congress Control Number: 2023947021

Printed in the United States of America

24 25 26 27 28 29 30 31 32 / BP / 10 9 8 7 6 5 4 3 2 1

Be joyful in hope, patient in affliction, faithful in prayer.
ROMANS 12:12

This book is dedicated to all those suffering
from multiple myeloma as well as their families.
May God in His infinite mercy provide
a cure for this disease.

. . . .

It is also dedicated to my friend Norman—
thank you for all the love, support, and prayers.
You hold a special place in my heart.

. . . .

Lastly, this book is dedicated to my husband, Rick—
my true love and my soulmate.
I couldn't do it without you!

Acknowledgments

A special thank you to my proofreaders, Rick, Thea, and Katy. Also, thank you to editors Kim Moore and Rod Morris for their professional guidance.

Contents

Introduction

Have you ever wished you could keep yourself and loved ones safe from danger? Perhaps you envision placing a protective bubble around the newest driver in the family or maybe figuring out a way for germs or cancer cells to bounce off those closest to you. For some, the desire may be not for physical protection but for safeguarding the hearts and minds of family members or friends during periods of personal difficulties.

I've been a volunteer emergency medical technician (EMT) on my town's first aid and rescue squad for 35 years, responding to more than 9,300 emergency calls. Along with my fellow squad members, I've been called to help those suffering cardiac arrest, victims of trauma from accidents, near-drownings, people suffering from drug overdoses, and a variety of other medical emergencies. We're blessed to be able to serve as instruments of God, acting as cogs in the wheel of heavenly orchestrated interventions. In my capacity as an EMT, I've observed firsthand how God carefully puts together all the pieces to create jaw-dropping, awe-inspiring rescues.

As an emergency medical services (EMS) volunteer, I meet people at their most vulnerable moments, when a seemingly ordinary day can suddenly morph into one that is dark and sinister, challenging their faith and calling into question an ongoing earthly existence versus transitioning to eternity with God. In these times of profound crisis, people turn to God for help. I know He hears our prayers, for I've seen them answered in ways that defy logic. His loving hand pulls us literally or figuratively to safety in ways that cannot be written off as mere chance.

"Wow, that was a lucky save!" some might say. I believe it's not luck at play but rather God's saving grace. The orchestrator of miracles, He puts all the pieces in motion to create occurrences that are truly beyond mere coincidence. In this book, I share my firsthand accounts of the ways God works to protect and save us. If we open our minds and hearts to the quiet presence of God in our lives, we'll be able to recognize these heavenly rescues.

Volunteer Members of the Pine Cove First Aid and Emergency Squad

Jessie Barnes—optometrist

Carl Blakely—businessman

Colin Branigan—actor with local theater group

Kerry Branson—architect

Kit Carmichael—financial advisor

Mason Chapman—auto mechanic

Clint Edwards—considering joining the armed forces

Jocelyn Farnsworth—bakery owner

Donna Ferlise—part-time florist

Colleen Harper—speech therapy student

Archie Harris—retired state employee

Helen McGuire—nurse

Ted O'Malley—retired national park service employee

Andrea Jo Rodgers (the author)— 35+ year volunteer on the rescue squad; physical therapist

Jose Sanchez—retired politician

Buddy Stone—retired pharmaceutical salesman

Kayla Taylor—retired dancer

Greg Turner—retired electrical engineer

Alec Waters—veterinary student

Darren Williams—retired army veteran

Members of the Pine Cove Police Department

Officer Ethan Bonilla

Officer Jack Endicott

Sergeant Derrick Flint

Dispatcher Jerome Franklin

Sergeant Kyle Jamieson

Officer Vinnie McGovern

Officer Brad Sims

Officer Pedro Suarez

Paramedics

Rose Anderson

Ty Fleming

William Moore

Paula Pritchard

Kennisha Smythe

Arthur Williamson

Chapter 1

Life at the End of a Yo-Yo String

Be strong and take heart,
all you who hope in the LORD.

PSALM 31:24

> **DISPATCHER:** "Request for the first aid squad at 600 Highway 65 for a two-year-old with an asthma attack."

As my first aid pager beeped, I glanced at the oven clock. My brownies had two minutes to go before they'd be finished baking. I felt bad, but I knew I couldn't respond to this call. We were already running late for Father's Day dinner at my sister Marie's house. As an emergency medical services volunteer, my family is used to me messing up holiday plans. It just goes with the territory. Marie planned to serve the meal in a few minutes. My husband, Rick, and our twins, Anna and John, were looking forward to it, and I was hoping not to spoil it. I knew we had other squad members available to help the victim with asthma.

I've been a volunteer emergency medical technician with the Pine Cove First Aid Squad for 35 years, responding to about 250 to 350 calls per year. We're a busy squad, responding to 1,000 first aid and fire calls each year. Our rescue squad includes approximately 25 members, ranging in age from 16-year-old cadets to those in their eighties. Since we live in a small town, we're able to respond to calls from our homes (or wherever we happen to be when we're dispatched) rather than stand by at our first aid building. When we're needed, our pagers are activated, and the dispatcher tells us the location and nature of the call. In addition, our cell phones have an app that notifies us of emergencies. Normally, it works out and we have more than enough members to respond to calls. I hoped a crew would call in service for the child with the asthma attack quickly. Otherwise, I'd be feeling mega-guilty.

Rick wandered into the kitchen, drawn by the rich chocolate scent floating from the oven. He's smart, hard-working, and has a sweet tooth. He can detect home-baked goodies from vast distances. "Why are you making brownies? Are you bringing those to Marie's house?"

"Yes, but they still need one more minute. Can you please tell the kids to get in the car?" Originally, Anna was supposed to have softball practice from 3:00 to 5:00 p.m. at the field on the other side of town. Her practice was canceled at the last minute (probably because the coach realized lots of families are firing up their grills for Father's Day), so I made a spur of the moment decision to start baking. I didn't realize it at the time, but God was already beginning to put the pieces in motion to create a miracle.

I watched as the oven timer ticked down the seconds. When there were still 15 left, I yanked the brownies out and tossed them onto a trivet on the counter. I like to be early for appointments and outings, and I'd told my sister we'd be there by a quarter to five. There was no chance of that happening.

I shoved the tray of brownies, still hot from the oven, into the back of our SUV. "Father's Day dinner, here we come," I said as I slipped into the driver's seat and pulled out of our garage.

As we approached the stop sign at the end of our street, my pager began chirping again. "Don't worry. I know I can't go," I said before my family could protest. "It's going to be a second request for a two-year-old with an asthma attack." I was dead wrong. The dispatcher's words startled me.

DISPATCHER: "Request for first aid at 720 Falcon Street for CPR in progress."

This wasn't another request for the pediatric call. It was a different address, about a mile from the first call. If someone was receiving cardiopulmonary resuscitation (CPR), that meant they were in cardiac arrest. They didn't have a heartbeat. They were clinically dead, necessitating urgent care for a chance at resuscitation.

I slammed on the brakes. "Sorry, but you have to get out. You can walk back home and take the other car to Marie's. Just eat without me."

Did I feel bad about throwing my husband and children out of the car? *Yes.* Fortunately, my family gets it. They understand the balance: sometimes family comes first, and other times first aid calls come first. Given the life and death nature of this alert, the first aid call took priority. No way would I eat dinner while someone's life hung in the balance.

I plugged my blue light into the cigarette lighter and flipped the switch on. Falcon Street was a mere three-quarters of a mile away. I decided it'd be faster to drive straight to the scene rather than two miles to our squad building. I figured some of the squad members who were responding to the asthma call would divert to the CPR call and meet me there with the ambulance. Rather than resetting my pager, I left the channel open so I could hear the transmissions of the rigs and dispatcher. I noted the dispatcher hadn't given much information about our patient. Was the victim a man or a woman? Young or old? I wondered if it was a witnessed arrest, meaning someone saw the person collapse. We have better odds of resuscitating people who have witnessed arrests with a short "down" time (period of time the person is without a pulse and not breathing before someone begins CPR).

When I got to Highway 65, I made a quick right turn and headed south. The pediatric asthma call was also on Highway 65, about a mile to the north. I glanced in my rearview mirror and noticed a Pine Cove police car coming up fast behind me. I pulled over to let him pass so he could lead the way to the CPR call. I glanced over as he drove by. I was glad to see Sergeant Kyle Jamieson, one of our finest men in blue. He's been a member of the police department for nearly as long as I've been a volunteer. He's also a certified EMT. We work together well as a team, and I couldn't think of anyone else I'd rather be with on this call.

Kyle recognized my car. "I'm being followed by a squad member to the scene," he told dispatch.

"Received," dispatcher Jerome Franklin replied. A veteran dispatcher, he always remains calm, even in dire emergencies.

"We're on the ramp," ambulance driver Clint Edwards notified Franklin. "We're diverting from the Highway 65 call and responding to the CPR call with a short crew. If we don't get additional members, you may need to call mutual aid to cover the asthma call."

Mutual aid means requesting a neighboring town's rescue squad to help. For example, if we have multiple calls at once or an accident with numerous victims, a nearby town will be called to give us a hand. Likewise, if they need help answering a call, we'll be dispatched to respond. This practice strengthens the fabric and resiliency of the volunteer EMS system.

Sergeant Jamieson turned left off the highway onto Falcon Street. A few blocks later, he parked in front of a well-kept beige Colonial with white shutters. I parked across the street, careful to leave room for our ambulance. I met Kyle at the open trunk of his patrol car. He grabbed the green jump kit and a defibrillator while I took the suction unit. We rushed along a red brick walkway, up a few front porch steps, and through the open door into a sunlit hall. A middle-aged woman with shoulder length brown hair and frightened eyes pointed toward the staircase. "They'll tell you what happened upstairs."

We hurried up the carpeted staircase. The clock was ticking, with each second that passed lessening our patient's chance of survival. About 90 percent of those who experience an out-of-the-hospital cardiac arrest die.

As I entered a large bedroom, I spotted a middle-aged man with short brown hair and an average build lying flat on his back on the floor, close to the foot of a king-size bed. The purplish-blue color of his face indicated he wasn't getting enough oxygen. He had agonal respirations, which are inadequate, reflexive, gasping-type breaths that people often make at the time of death.

A young woman knelt on the right side of the gentleman, performing chest compressions. Another young woman stood next to her, clutching a cordless phone. I assumed they were the man's daughters. A 911 operator was giving instructions via speakerphone on how to properly administer CPR.

Kyle and I knelt on the man's left side. I palpated the side of his neck for a carotid pulse. "No pulse."

Kyle deftly attached the defibrillation electrodes to the machine, pushed the unit toward me, and took over performing chest compressions. I placed the defibrillation pads on our victim's chest, turned on the unit, and pressed the analyze button.

Our squad carries semiautomatic defibrillators (SAEDs). Once you attach an SAED's electrodes and turn the unit on, it announces directions. In this case, the unit instructed "Shock advised."

"Everyone clear," I said, waving my arm over the man's body to make sure no one was touching him. If a person contacts the victim when he's defibrillated, you end up with two victims. Just as a shock from an SAED can start a heart that has stopped, it can also stop a heart that is beating. The machine charged up with a loud whirring noise. I pressed the shock button and powerful joules of energy coursed through our patient, causing his body to jerk.

"Low battery warning," the machine advised. How many times could the machine shock before it ran out of juice? I didn't want to find out. "Kyle, can you tell the rig to bring our defibrillator up?" I knew they most likely would anyway but didn't want to take any chances.

Kyle nodded and keyed the mike on his shoulder to relay the message to Clint.

Since I'd left my pager channel open, I could hear Clint speaking with dispatcher Franklin. "Should I send Marina Beach police to assist with the call?" Franklin asked Clint.

"No, send Sandy Springs. They're closer," Clint replied.

Sandy Springs is a small town just to our south. *That's good. We'll have additional defibrillators if ours runs out of battery power.* I took a deep breath and performed chest compressions at a rate of 100 per minute. My adrenalin surging, I reminded myself not to pump too fast. Ironically, our first aid squad recertified in CPR less than a week ago.

Kyle hooked the bag valve mask (BVM) to a portable oxygen tank. A BVM is a handheld device used to provide positive pressure ventilations (i.e., breaths) to a person who isn't breathing or who has inadequate respiratory effort. Hooking the BVM tubing to an oxygen tank allows us to supply 100 percent oxygen instead of the normal 21 percent in room air. The mask is placed over the patient's nose and mouth. The rescuer squeezes the bag portion (similar to a football) just enough to allow the patient's chest to rise. Kyle began squeezing the BVM, deftly administering rescue breaths and sending much-needed oxygen into the man's lungs. We worked as a team, providing chest compressions and rescue breaths.

I glanced up at the women. "Can you tell us what happened?"

The daughter who knelt on the floor next to us spoke first. "I'm Jenna and this is our father, Scott Williams. We just got home from Father's Day lunch. My dad said he felt very full. I told him I'd get him a glass of water. I wasn't out of the room ten seconds when I heard a crash." She paused to take a deep breath. "When I rushed back in, I found Dad on the floor. When I called his name and shook his shoulder, he didn't respond. I could tell he wasn't breathing. I called my sister, Colleen, to help."

Colleen, visibly upset, stepped forward. "I called 911 and yelled down to my mother to come up. The 911 dispatcher told us she was sending an ambulance. She told us how to check Dad's pulse. Since we couldn't feel one, she told us to start pressing on his chest. We've never done CPR before. I hope we did it right."

"You did fantastic," Sergeant Jamieson replied. Just then, Sandy Springs police officer Alejandro Cabello entered and handed Kyle an SAED. Kyle switched defibrillators and pressed the analyze button. *No shock advised.*

Officer Cabello assisted Kyle by keeping Scott's airway open with a head tilt/chin lift maneuver. This technique is used to open an unconscious person's airway by tilting the head back into a hyperextended position with one hand and gently lifting the chin with the other hand. It helps prevent the tongue from blocking the airway. We use this maneuver when we don't suspect neck trauma.

Scott had been without a pulse for about five minutes. Why wasn't the defibrillator recommending a second shock? Was he in asystole (flatline)? Defibrillators don't work for asystole. I worried his chances at resuscitation could be slipping away like petals from a wilting rose. *One, two, three, four, five, six.* Silently, I counted chest compressions and kept pumping on Scott's chest. I glanced at his face. It seemed less blue. The oxygen appeared to be helping.

"Press to analyze," the defibrillator instructed. Kyle re-pressed the analyze button. "Press to shock," the machine coached. Since the SAED was recommending another shock, I thought Scott could be in ventricular fibrillation (V-fib), a heart rhythm marked by ineffective contractions caused by abnormal electrical activity. Instead of a body organ with regular, normal contractions, picture the heart as a bag full of squirming worms.

Kyle pressed the button, and once again, hundreds of joules of energy poured into Scott's chest. I prayed the shock would convert his fatal cardiac arrythmia back to a normal one.

Two more Sandy Springs police officers, Ned Kearns and Reefe Albertson, rushed into the bedroom. *Good. More help.* A focused current of tension filled the room as we worked feverishly to bring back Scott.

"Alejandro, can we switch, and you take over compressions?" I asked. He nodded and slid closer to me, ready to take my place when I finished my set of thirty. Once he took over, I switched from Scott's right side to his left. I fished a set of oropharyngeal airways out of Sergeant Jamieson's first aid jump kit and pulled one from the center of the box. Oropharyngeal airways, also called oral airways or OPA for short, help to maintain an open airway by preventing the tongue from covering the epiglottis. I measured it from the tip of Scott's ear to the corner of his mouth and inserted it into his mouth, careful to rotate it 180 degrees as I put it in.

Once I finished, Kyle passed me the BVM. "You can take over breaths." He placed two fingers along Scott's carotid artery. "Hey, I've got a strong pulse. Hold compressions."

My heart filled with hope. *Come on, Scott, fight. You have a wonderful wife and two beautiful daughters who love and need you.* I continued performing rescue breathing, squeezing the BVM once every five seconds. I glanced at Jenna. She knelt about five feet away, stared intently at her father's face, willing the man who helped give her life to live. Her mother entered the room, eyes filled with tears. She and Colleen embraced.

"We've lost pulses. Start compressions again," Sergeant Jamieson said. Officer Cabello placed his clasped hands on Scott's sternum and resumed pressing down on his chest.

Scott's life hung at the end of a yo-yo string, flirting between continuing life on Earth versus transitioning to the afterlife. At this point, it was hard to tell where he would ultimately land, but for the sake of his family, I was praying for Earth.

Chapter 2

The Father's Day Miracle

For it is by grace you have been saved, through faith —
and this is not from yourselves, it is the gift of God.

EPHESIANS 2:8

Sergeant Jamieson pressed the analyze button on the defibrillator again. "Shock advised," the machine directed. Swiftly, he pressed the shock button.

I held by breath. *Come on, Scott. You can do this.* This would be his third shock. Isn't three supposed to be a charm? Sadly, in this case, it wasn't. Scott's pulse remained absent. In other words, he stayed clinically dead.

We resumed CPR, with Officer Cabello continuing chest compressions, Kyle keeping Scott's airway open, and with me squeezing the BVM. Within a minute, our Pine Cove ambulance crew arrived. Clint Edwards entered the room, accompanied by Kerry Branson and Colin Branigan. Kerry works as an architect but spends some of her free time volunteering with our squad. Colin works part time as a chef at one of our local eateries.

I noticed a bit of vomit on Scott's upper lip. "Kerry, can you set up the suction for me?"

Kerry began attaching the suction tubing to the unit and running a little sterile water through the set-up.

"My dad vomited a little while I was pressing on his chest. Is that normal?" Jenna asked.

I nodded. "Especially since he just ate."

Colin set our first aid jump kit on the floor. "What can I do to help?"

"You can switch the oxygen tank. It's getting low," I replied. Scott was getting 15 liters of oxygen per minute. At that rate, portable oxygen tanks empty quickly.

"Got it. I'll have the backboard ready in the hallway and the cot set up downstairs," he said.

"Thanks." I paused from providing rescue breaths to briefly suction Scott's airway. Using a Yankauer catheter (a rigid-tipped catheter), I used a figure-eight technique to suction within Scott's mouth for 15 seconds. Suctioning helps prevent complications such as aspiration pneumonia.

As Colin exited the room, paramedics Rose Anderson and William Moore entered. In our region, volunteers give basic life support (BLS) and paramedics are employees of the hospital. They provide advanced life support (ALS) such as intravenous lines, administering numerous medications, applying and interpreting electrocardiograms, and performing intubation. Intubation is the process in which an endotracheal tube (ET tube) is inserted through the person's mouth into their airway. We can then hook the BVM mask directly to the end of the ET tube. It makes it easier to ventilate the patient and helps ensure the oxygen enters the airway and lungs rather than the stomach.

I'd been concerned the paramedics would be delayed responding to this call or maybe even not be available at all. I knew medics were dispatched to the pediatric asthma call on Highway 65. I figured they'd have to call a second unit from a farther-away hospital to help us. I wasn't sure how they got here this quickly, but I was thrilled.

"What's his down time?" William asked, sliding in next to me at Scott's head. He began pulling intubation materials from his airway jump kit. William spent many years as an accountant before making a career change to paramedic. He says he prefers his new job because numbers can't talk the same way people can.

"His down time is close to zero. His daughters started chest compressions almost immediately," Sergeant Jamieson said.

Rose Anderson became William's partner years ago when she relocated to our state from Iowa. She traded farm fields for ocean breezes. She attached cardiac electrodes to Scott's chest and studied the heart monitor. "I've got v-tach. I'm going to shock."

V-tach stands for ventricular tachycardia. The heart has two upper chambers (atria) and two lower chambers (ventricles). V-tach is an arrhythmia that involves abnormal electrical signals in the ventricles. The heart beats too fast and in a chaotic manner, which means the heart chambers can't adequately fill with blood. When this occurs, there's not enough blood to send to the heart, lungs, and rest of the body.

Rose turned our SAED off and switched to her own defibrillation pads. "Everybody clear," she said, holding one defibrillation paddle in each hand. When she was sure none of us had physical contact with Scott, she touched the paddles to his chest and shocked him.

That's four shocks! A lot of juice to pump into someone. William finished intubating Scott. "You can start squeezing again once every five seconds," he directed me.

Rose started an IV line and administered several medications, such as epinephrine. Hopefully, the drugs would help to jumpstart Scott's heart again.

"Is that a medic alert tag around his neck?" William asked.

I lifted the silver medallion from Scott's chest and peered at it closely. "It's a religious medal." I gave it a quick squeeze and offered a silent prayer, *Help, God.*

Rose held up her hand. "Pause compressions." She placed her fingers on the side of Scott's neck. "I've got a strong carotid."

William passed me a blood-pressure cuff. "I'll take over bagging him. I want you to get a pressure."

I crawled from Scott's head to his side and felt his wrist. "He's got a strong radial pulse too." That's a good sign. It meant Scott's systolic blood pressure (the top number) was at least 80. I wrapped the cuff around his upper arm and inflated it. "His pressure is 170 over 108."

Kyle, Alejandro, and I rolled Scott to his side and placed a backboard next to him, then rolled him back and strapped him in. We'd need the board to carry him downstairs. I used two cravats to loop around his feet and then tied them to the backboard, thus securing them in place so his body wouldn't slide downwards on the staircase.

Kyle, Colin, Alejandro, and Officer Albertson worked together to carry Scott down the staircase. Clint backed them up, calling out how many stairs were left to ensure they kept their footing. Kerry picked up the SAED and followed them. I slung the strap to our jump kit over my shoulder and picked up the two suction units. Scott's family hung back, waiting for all of us to step out of the bedroom. My heart filled with empathy. "You did a really great job by starting CPR so quickly," I said. Without their quick actions, their father's chances for survival would be much lower.

"Thank you for saying that. Can I ride to the hospital in the ambulance?" Jenna asked.

"Yes, you can have the front seat. Just to make sure, you said your dad has no past medical history, no medications, and no allergies to medications, right?"

"Yes, that's right. Dad's always been super-healthy," Jenna said. "It's hard to believe this is happening."

"I'll drive us, Mom," Colleen said. Mrs. Williams grasped her daughter's forearm and nodded, too upset to speak.

I hurried down the stairs, as fast as you can hurry when you're carrying heavy equipment. When I reached the last step, I saw Scott being lifted onto our stretcher. I slipped past them and headed to the ambulance. I turned on the onboard oxygen and suction so it would be ready to use.

Clint helped Jenna settle into the front passenger seat and then sat next to her in the driver's seat. Colin climbed in the back with me, along with medic William. I switched the portable oxygen to our onboard tank while William hung the IV line from a clip on the rig's ceiling. Soon, we were ready to start our journey to the hospital. I sat in the captain's chair at the head of the stretcher. William signaled for me to take over squeezing the BVM so he could attend to Scott's other needs.

I glanced at Jenna, who watched from the front seat. Her face wore a jumble of emotions: hope, fear, sadness. Her hands were clasped together, and I could see she was praying.

"When we get to the hospital, we'll go straight back to the main emergency department," I said. "They'll have a team of people waiting for your dad." Jenna nodded, trying to process how a beautiful afternoon with her family had suddenly turned so dark and frightening.

I studied Scott's face. He remained unresponsive, not attempting to take any breaths on his own. However, his heart continued to pump steadily. His short brown hair and lean, muscular physique gave him a youthful appearance that belied his current condition. I smoothed his hair back. "Scott, your daughter Jenna is sitting in the front seat. We're almost at the hospital. Hang in there." I wasn't sure if he could hear me, but I hoped, on some level, he would understand my words of encouragement.

Clint backed the ambulance into a parking space in the hospital garage so we could unload Scott. "Once we get to the room, they may ask you to wait in the hallway," I said to Jenna. "There's going to be a lot of activity going on." She swallowed and nodded. The next leg of the journey was beginning.

Triage nurse Maggie Summers met us at the entrance. She'd been a pillar in the emergency department (ED) for decades. Knowledgeable and self-assured, she kept things running smoothly. She peered at Scott, her brows furrowed with concern. "Good job getting his pulse back. Room 23 is ready for you. Just do me a favor and register him at the desk first."

I paused at the registration desk to give Scott's information, while the rest of our team rolled the stretcher down the long hallway toward the back of the ED. William kept squeezing the BVM, providing Scott with oxygen-rich ventilations. I kept hoping Scott would begin breathing on his own. Wake up. Live.

I caught up with our team just as they lifted Scott from our stretcher to the hospital's. I detangled the IV line and hung it on a hook at the corner of the stretcher. Through the curtain, I caught a glimpse of Jenna sitting in a chair in the hallway. I know what it's like to sit in that chair as a family member. My heart clenched for her.

I refocused my attention on Scott. Many people entered the room. William explained the events to the ED physician, Dr. Morgan. He's knowledgeable and an expert in emergency medicine. We'd done our part by transitioning Scott's care into capable hands. Dr. Morgan began rattling off instructions to the staff. I switched the oxygen tubing from our portable tank to the hospital's wall unit. A respiratory therapist rolled a ventilator (life support machine) into the examination room. As the nurses cared for Scott, I silently backed out of the room into the hallway. I found a small piece of scrap paper on the counter and scribbled my name and cell phone number on it.

Jenna leaned forward on the rigid plastic chair, her fingers gripping the sides as she waited for news from Dr. Morgan. I handed her the slip of paper with my contact information. "I know you have a lot on your mind, but if it's not too much trouble and you feel up to it, could you please keep us posted?"

Jenna nodded. "Of course. Thank you for everything all of you did today."

I gave her a quick hug. "You and your sister are amazing."

"Thank you." She folded the piece of paper and slipped it into her pocket. "I'll be in touch."

. . . .

My thoughts stayed with Jenna and her family throughout the evening. I'm an optimist. The kind of person who sees a glass as half-full instead of half-empty. But even I had to acknowledge the gravity of Scott's situation. His odds of survival seemed slim.

After we cleaned and disinfected the rig, and replaced the equipment we'd used on the call, I finally headed to my sister's house for a very belated Father's Day dinner. "I'm so sorry," I said as I stepped into her house, holding the tray of brownies as a peace offering.

Marie smiled. "Don't worry about it. We're used to it. I saved you a plate."

"How's the person? Did you save them?" John asked. He and Anna plan to join Pine Cove First Aid Squad as cadets when they turn 16.

I placed the brownies on the kitchen counter. "We did, but he's not out of the woods. He needs lots of prayers." I appreciated how fortunate I was to be spending Father's Day (despite the delay) with my family.

Later that night, when my squad and I brought a 91-year-old male with weakness and diarrhea to the ED, our crew returned to Room 23 to check on Scott. The room was empty. No sign of him. Had he passed away? I couldn't bear the thought. I knew his condition had been precarious when we left him. I spotted a nurse. "Do you know what happened to the man in Room 23?"

"I have no idea. I just got on duty an hour ago. That room's been empty for a while."

An ED tech entering vital signs into a nearby computer looked up when he overheard our question. "I'm pretty sure that man went up to the floor."

That meant Scott made it to the coronary care unit (CCU). *He's still alive!*

. . . .

The next day, Clint and I ran into Sergeant Jamieson and Officer Pedro Suarez outside of police headquarters after they returned from a burglary alarm call. Kyle had been with Pedro at the pediatric asthma call yesterday until he broke away to respond to the CPR call for Scott Williams. Pedro, a recent addition to the police force, remained with the child, providing care until EMS arrived.

"It was lucky we had the medics for our asthma call. We didn't need them, so I was able to send them directly to the CPR call. By having them already in our town, it saved a lot of time and got them to where they were needed much faster," Pedro said.

"How incredibly fortunate," I said. The paramedics cover a large area. Sometimes, they respond from 15 to 20 minutes away. Other times, they aren't available at all. For example, if the local paramedics (William and Rose) had been needed on the asthma call, they would have had to dispatch a different pair of medics from a farther away location. Sometimes, if the medics are coming from the opposite direction of where we're travelling and they're more than 15 minutes away, we end up having to cancel them because we'd already be at the hospital by the time they arrived. *God's hand at work. Putting the paramedics only one mile away when Scott and his family needed them.* "Any word on how he's doing?"

Kyle nodded. "He had open heart surgery last night. I think it was a three-vessel bypass surgery. I heard his LAD was 99 or 100 percent occluded." LAD stands for left anterior descending artery. It supplies a large amount of the heart with oxygenated blood. When it becomes occluded, it's often deadly. That's why it's often referred to as "the widow maker."

"Right now, he's paralyzed and sedated, so the doctor's unsure of his neurological status," Kyle continued. "His troponin level is high, which could indicate he has cardiac muscle damage." It's common for critically ill patients who are intubated and on ventilators to be paralyzed and sedated with medications.

"It's encouraging he survived the surgery," Clint said.

"It sure is." I prayed Scott would wake up and that his heart muscle wasn't permanently damaged. It struck me it wasn't just the location of the paramedics that had been a blessing. If my daughter's softball practice hadn't been canceled, I would have been miles away on the other side of town when the call went out. Instead, I was already in my car, just a brief ride away.

Kyle rocked back on his heels. "You know, I wasn't even supposed to be on duty yesterday."

Clint's eyes widened. "Really?"

"One of the guys has a newborn. He wanted to celebrate his first Father's Day with the baby, so I switched shifts with him."

Another small miracle. Kyle and I have been answering calls together for decades, working together seamlessly. God strung together many pieces for Scott to get this far. Now, we just needed the miracle to keep rolling forward.

. . . .

Over the next several days I thought of Scott and his family often. Had he opened his eyes? Was he still on a ventilator? Would his life ever be the same?

I'm a physical therapist. Sometimes I work in the hospital, but usually I'm in an outpatient facility across the street from where Scott had his heart surgery. On the Wednesday following our first aid call for him, as I sat in our staff room preparing to eat lunch, I noticed a voicemail on my cell phone. I didn't recognize the number. Just as I pressed the play button, the room got noisy. I could tell it was a woman leaving the message, but the only words I caught were "woke up." Dare I hope? Could it be Scott's daughter? Or was it just another telemarketer?

I slipped into a quiet room to listen to the voicemail. It was Jenna! Joy filled me as I listened to her words.

"Hi, this is Jenna Williams. You were helping my dad Sunday night. I just wanted to update you and let you know how he's doing. He woke up today! He is completely responsive and knows who we are and is talking with us. We just wanted to thank you so much for helping us to make this happen. Please tell everyone thank you so much for all you did."

I glanced at my watch. I had time to run over to the hospital and visit him. My Swiss cheese on rye sandwich could wait. I knew Scott must be in the cardiac wing of the critical care unit for postsurgical patients. The unit secretary looked up from typing and smiled. "How can I help you?"

"I'm here to visit Scott Williams," I said, trying to contain my excitement. She pointed me down the hall. "Second room on your left."

I paused outside the room and peeked in through the glass windows. The man I saw now looked markedly different from the one I did CPR on the other night. This one looked healthy, vibrant, *alive*. A young male nurse wearing navy-blue scrubs sat outside Scott's room, charting on a portable computer.

Part of me couldn't believe this man was truly Scott. Just to be sure, I asked the nurse to confirm he was indeed Scott Williams. He smiled. "He sure is."

I gazed at Scott intently. I noticed a small laceration above his right eyebrow. I figured he must have gotten that when he fell. He was no longer on a ventilator but rather a simple nasal cannula. A heart monitor kept track of his cardiac rate and rhythm. An intravenous line delivered fluid and medication into his left arm. Overall, he looked alert and comfortable. *Amazing.*

I hesitated at the doorway, watching as he used the remote control to flip through channels on the wall-mounted television. Just as I was about to enter, a cardiac surgeon stepped past me into the room. I took a step back, wishing to give Scott privacy.

A few minutes later, the surgeon stepped back out of Scott's room. He caught sight of me and asked, "Are you family?"

I smiled. "No, I'm with the first aid squad."

"Were you one of the ones who did CPR on Mr. Williams?"

I nodded. "He looks so different now."

"I bet!" The doctor stepped back into Scott's room. "You have a visitor. Here's one of the people who saved your life." He smiled and waved goodbye.

I entered the room slowly. It felt almost surreal that this was happening. CPR saves are rare, especially ones that result in people who can talk and walk out of the hospital. I approached his bed. Now that I was here, I wasn't exactly sure what to say. I blurted out, "My name is Andrea. I'm with the first aid squad. You look much better than the last time I saw you."

A bright smile lit his face. "Thank goodness for that."

"Are you in pain? You must be sore." I imagined the chest compressions coupled with the surgery may have made his ribcage painful.

Scott shook his head. "I feel great. No pain at all. I feel like I could just get up and start walking."

"That's terrific. Well, your daughters are wonderful. They did CPR on you. A lot of people wouldn't have been able to do that. They're the ones who truly saved you that day." By providing immediate chest compressions, they helped to ensure that oxygen kept circulating in Scott's brain, preventing anoxic brain damage.

"I imagine it was a real team effort. I want to thank all of you." Scott noticed my name badge. "Do you work here?"

I explained how I occasionally work in the hospital, but more often in the outpatient division across the street. "I used to work in the hospital with open heart patients before I had my children." After we had chatted a few minutes about recovering from bypass surgery, Scott's mother, wife, brother, and two daughters entered the room.

I hugged Jenna tightly. "Your voicemail message made my entire year!" I hugged Mrs. Williams and Colleen too, feeling awed that God blessed me by letting me take part in this miraculous rescue.

Scott sucked on an ice chip. "You know, I don't remember anything about that afternoon. I remember going to church that morning. I know we went out to lunch to celebrate Father's Day, but I don't remember where. It was probably the usual place we go, but I couldn't swear to it."

Laura stroked Scott's arm. "You guessed right. We went to our usual spot, Whale of a Good Time."

"What did I eat? The crab cake sandwich?"

Jenna smiled. "Of course."

"Remind me not to get that if I go there," I joked. "But seriously, you did an incredible job. By staying calm and following the directions of the 911 operator, you truly saved your dad's life. What an incredible Father's Day gift."

"And we must have pulled you away from your own Father's Day," Scott said.

I laughed as I explained how I threw my family out of our car and told them to walk home. "They're used to it by now." I related how Anna's softball practice was canceled, allowing me to be in the right place at the right time. I told them how I pulled over for Kyle so he could lead the way to their home with lights and sirens.

"The two of you really click. You make a great team," Colleen said.

"Everything went so smoothly," Jenna added.

I nodded. "Even having the paramedics so quickly. They were at a first aid call just a mile away, and the police officer released them and sent them to you instead. They intubated you right away and gave you heart medications."

Scott whistled. "Amazing."

"We can go for hours or even days without another call. Having the other first aid call just a few minutes before yours put everything in motion to get help to you faster."

Just then, the cardiac surgeon returned. "Scott is doing fantastic. He'll be here in the intensive care unit for another day or two and then transfer to a step-down telemetry unit. After that, depending on how he's doing, he'll either go home or to a rehab facility. After a month or so, he can start outpatient cardiac rehab."

"That sounds like a great plan. Thank you so much," Scott said.

"I've never seen anything like this in my thirty years. It's a miracle that your daughters could do such successful CPR without ever having done it before," the surgeon said.

After the doctor left, I said, "I noticed the medal around your neck while I was doing CPR. At first, I thought it might be a medic alert tag but then realized it's a religious medal."

"That's St. Christopher. I've worn that medal since I was three or four years old."

"When I picked it up to see if it was a medical tag and realized it was religious, I gave it a quick squeeze with a very simple prayer…*Help*."

Jenna pointed upwards. "Thank goodness. God was listening and heard our prayers."

That magical save marked some of the happiest moments in my entire volunteer EMT career. On that day, many small miracles connected together to enable an incredible Father's Day rescue.

Chapter 3

Miracle on the Tracks

Jesus looked at them and said, "With man this is impossible,
but with God all things are possible."

MATTHEW 19:26

The whiskey in young Benjamin Wadsworth's belly impaired his senses, dulled his thoughts, slowed his reaction time. He didn't notice. Nor did he care.

That is, he didn't care until he spotted flashing lights in the distance. He was just sober enough to realize he was intoxicated. Loaded. D-R-U-N-K. Aware enough to know if he got pulled over, he'd be toast. No way could he walk a straight line right now. He'd be convicted of DWI for sure. He couldn't risk it. No way was he losing his driver's license. Not to mention, he was leaving for vacation in two days. Sun-filled sandy beaches were in his future, not a jail cell.

Benjamin didn't have a clear handle on where he was. He'd been to a few bars already tonight. This highway didn't look familiar. He eyed some no-name gas stations, several banks, a hair-styling salon, a real estate office, and a few mom-and-pop restaurants. None of them rang a bell. As he got closer to the flashing lights, he noticed a police officer had some guy pulled over on the opposite side of the street. Maybe the cop would be too busy to notice him.

Benjamin's inebriated condition clouded his judgement. He decided the best way to slip past undetected would be to floor it.

Pressing down on the accelerator, he sped by the cop. He figured since the officer was busy ticketing that guy, he couldn't just leave him to chase after someone else.

Or could he? Benjamin wasn't sure how that worked. What if the cop stayed with the car he pulled over, but radioed for someone else to go after him? He'd better get outta here, while the getting was good. He made a hard right at the next traffic light, careening off the highway onto a side street.

Benjamin didn't see the dark sedan parked on the right side of the street. *Scrape, scrape, scrape.* The screeching metallic noise roused his senses. *Hey, where'd that car jump out from?* He overcompensated by jerking his wheel to the left and pressed down on the accelerator.

Wham! What the heck is that? Benjamin rolled down his window and peered outside. Wouldn't you know it? Somehow, a parked car must have hit him. A guy in his forties stood near the SUV. He didn't look happy. What nerve. After all, Benjamin reasoned, that guy's car just hit me. "Don't worry about it. I'm okay," he called out to the man and kept rolling.

"Hey, you hit my car!" the man yelled. Benjamin didn't hear him. He'd already rolled his window back up and was cruising eastward. If people didn't keep slowing him down, he worried he'd be pulled over for sure.

. . . .

Cory Needle yanked his cell phone out of his rear pocket and snapped a photo of the license plate of the guy who just hit his car. *What a jerk! He hits my car, tells me he's okay and not to worry about it, and takes off.*

Cory rushed up his driveway to go inside and tell his wife. In the darkness, he tripped over a garden hose and landed hard on his hands and knees. Still clutching his cell phone, he dialed his wife's number. "You better come outside quick. I'm on the driveway…"

. . . .

DISPATCHER to Pine Cove Police Units: "Report of a hit-and-run on Chambers Street just south of Highway 65. A dark-colored SUV hit a parked vehicle. The caller reports the driver of the vehicle appears to be intoxicated. SUV last seen heading east on Chambers Street. Stand by for license plate number."

Sergeant Kyle Jamieson flipped on his emergency lights. "I'm responding." He was only about a mile from Chambers Street.

Sergeant Derrick Flint, who just finished handling a motor vehicle stop at the other end of Pine Cove, also began searching for the vehicle. A fifteen-year veteran of the department, he was known for his dedication and strong work ethic.

Officer Jack Endicott quickly wrapped up a vandalism report and joined in the search. Being a police officer ran in his blood. His father and grandfather had served as police officers too.

DISPATCHER: "Be advised, a Sandy Springs police officer reports an SUV matching that description sped by him heading north on Route 65 while he was on a traffic stop several minutes ago."

. . . .

Benjamin's hands grew sweaty. *Do I hear police sirens? Am I imagining them?* He wasn't taking any chances. He turned right off Chambers Street, then made the first left onto a quiet tree-lined street.

Bang! What the heck was that? Puzzled, Benjamin briefly came to a stop. Can you imagine? Another parked car somehow hit him. Bad timing, what with the police chasing him.

Benjamin turned off his headlights to make his SUV less visible to the cops. Then he floored it. Going 60 mph in a 25 zone, he felt confident he'd lose the police in no time.

Initially, the plan seemed to be working. Benjamin released a long, pent-up breath. It had looked dicey there for a few minutes, but now he felt everything was going to work out okay. *Caribbean beach, here I come!*

Since his headlights were turned off, Benjamin didn't realize he was driving on a dead-end street. Faster and faster, his car raced eastward. The tremendous impact of his vehicle striking the barricade marking the end of Chestnut Street wiped the smile from his face and replaced it with a burgeoning sense of horror. Suddenly, he experienced a sensation of weightlessness as his car launched through the air.

His car landed with a violent thud in an area of pitch blackness.

Benjamin took a second to assess his plight. He found it almost incredible to believe, but somehow, he was still alive. In fact, nothing even hurt that bad. But he was pretty sure his car wasn't drivable anymore. Serious bummer. He'd have to continue his escape from the cops on foot. He felt the effects of the liquor wearing off and a bad headache coming on.

He pulled the lever of his car door to push it open, but it wouldn't budge. *That figures, with the way tonight is going. What else could go wrong?* Benjamin reached over to open the passenger-side door. He fumbled in the darkness to find the lever, but that door was stuck shut too. The impact must have really done a number on his vehicle.

Suddenly, Benjamin heard the long blast of a horn. He knew that sound. The contents of his stomach threatened to explode from his mouth. It was a train whistle.

His SUV, seconds earlier submerged in total darkness, now became illuminated by the headlights from an approaching passenger train. He'd landed directly on the train tracks! Benjamin looked up at the giant black monster in terror as it bore down on him. Nowhere to go. No way to escape. No time to try climbing out the back of the SUV. The sound of the train's whistle grew louder as it raced closer. It seemed to shriek, "GET OFF THE TRACKS!"

The SUV began vibrating. A feeling of finality washed over him. It would take nothing short of a divine miracle to spare his life now. Benjamin Wadsworth was pretty sure he was about to meet his Maker.

. . . .

DISPATCHER: "Request for patrols and first aid at the Chestnut Street railroad crossing for a car struck by a train."

Sergeant Kyle Jamieson parked in front of the barricade at the end of Chestnut Street. Pulling his flashlight from his belt, he strode around the barricade, pausing at the line of large stones that marked the beginning of railroad property. He shined a beam of light across the accident scene. A crumpled SUV lay on the southbound tracks. Numerous wires were strewn across the ground, intermingled with wreckage from the vehicle. He took great care to avoid stepping on them.

Kyle heard the hum of the train's engine further down the tracks, in the direction of Sandy Springs. At the speed the train had been going, he realized it must have taken the engineer several blocks to safely halt it after the impact. He shined his flashlight toward the SUV. A large pole rested across the roof of the vehicle. He shifted the beam of light to the driver's side, noting the massive intrusion of the metal door into the compartment. *Empty.* If the driver had remained in the driver's seat, he'd most certainly be dead. He swept his flashlight across the passenger side. *Also empty.* He checked the rear section of the SUV…or, more precisely, what was left of it. Again, no victim to be found.

Officer Jack Endicott and Sergeant Derrick Flint joined Kyle at the scene. "Watch out for the wires," Kyle shouted. Just then, he heard a soft moan. Almost in disbelief, he realized the victim must still be alive. But where was he? He noticed the rear window was shattered. Kyle theorized he must have been ejected from the vehicle from the sheer force of the impact. He pointed his flashlight to the area behind the SUV. Still nothing. He dropped down onto his hands and knees, shining his light underneath the vehicle. *Bingo.*

Beneath the rear of the SUV, a young man lay unconscious, barely clinging to life. "Radio dispatch that I've found him under his car," Kyle said. "He's unconscious. I'll check to see if he has a pulse."

The three worked as a team to slide Benjamin out from underneath the SUV. Since the SUV could catch on fire, they carefully carried him off the tracks to safety.

. . . .

I awoke with a start to the sound of my pager. Car struck by a train? It sounded bad. I slipped on my sneakers, grabbed my first aid hoodie, and hustled out the door. As I climbed into my car, I heard Colin Branigan tell dispatch, "We're on the ramp." I realized he and new member Donna Ferlise, a part-time florist, must still be at the building from an earlier call. Knowing I wouldn't make the rig, and since the accident wasn't far from where I live, I headed toward Chestnut Street.

DISPATCHER: "Update—patient is unconscious at this time."

I parked on the east side of the railroad tracks, walked around the dead-end barricade, and climbed up a small incline of rocks. A police officer from a neighboring town directed me to cross over. "They've pulled the victim into the road on the other side," he said.

I took great care stepping over the tracks. A blinding light shone in my eyes, making it challenging to see. I figured it must be the headlights from numerous police cars. As I made my way across, I wondered about our patient's condition. It's not that uncommon for our squad to respond to first aid calls on the railroad tracks. But it's *extremely* uncommon for the patients to survive. Usually, they are determined to be dead on arrival (DOA). The police often cancel us before we ever touch the patient.

I slipped around the black-and-white barricade and found our victim, an unconscious young man with shoulder-length brown hair, flat on his back on the pavement, surrounded by Sergeant Jamieson, Sergeant Flint, and Officer Endicott. The dusky-gray color of his face pointed to the severity of his condition. He had a deep gash above his right eyebrow and road rash from his left elbow to wrist. Blood streaked his face, dark-gray T-shirt, and ripped jeans. The police had already applied a cervical collar to stabilize his spine. They'd also placed him on high-flow oxygen via a non-rebreather mask.

"We were able to get his ID from his wallet. He's a 29-year-old male—Benjamin Wadsworth. He has no major bleeding, but his respiratory status is deteriorating," Sergeant Jamieson said. "He was struck by a train and ejected from his vehicle. The SUV then landed on top of him, and he was wedged underneath it."

I grimaced. "That's horrible."

I noticed Benjamin now had agonal respirations, which are reflexive gasping breaths. Agonal breathing isn't true breathing. It's a sign that the brain is still alive but not getting enough oxygen. This type of respiration often indicates a person is near death. We'd have to start assisting Benjamin's breathing to increase his odds of survival.

"Do you have oral airways in your kit?" I asked.

Sergeant Flint pulled a case of airways from his green jump kit. "Here you go."

"While I size this, can you set up a BVM?" I pulled a size 10 airway from the case and measured it from the tip of Benjamin's ear to the corner of his mouth. He didn't appear to have any oral trauma, so I carefully inserted the airway. *No gag reflex. He's completely out.*

Officer Endicott continued holding cervical stabilization on Benjamin's head and neck, manually opening his airway with a modified jaw thrust, a technique first responders use when a neck injury is suspected. I placed the BVM (bag valve mask) over Benjamin's face and began squeezing the bag portion once every five seconds.

Sergeant Jamieson rechecked Benjamin's pulse. "It's holding at 110, weak but regular."

As I continued squeezing the BVM, it seemed almost incomprehensible that this man was still alive. The gray hue of his face gradually shifted to a pale white.

"Hey, he's starting to move his right leg a bit," Sergeant Jamieson said. "The ambulance is about a minute out, and the medics have a five-minute ETA."

I glanced at Benjamin's right leg. *It's definitely moving.* He began kicking his left leg too. Then he batted away the BVM and yanked out the oral airway. "Benjamin, it's okay. You're going to be all right," I said, trying to soothe him.

Sergeant Flint passed the non-rebreather mask back to me. While Officer Endicott kept holding cervical stabilization, I slipped the oxygen mask onto Benjamin's face. "Keep this on. It's going to help you."

Benjamin grunted. Although he kept squirming, he didn't try to pull off the mask. A few seconds later, Helen McGuire appeared at my side. I admire Helen greatly; she somehow balances working as a nurse, caring for her family, and volunteering on the rescue squad. Jessie Barnes and Donna Ferlise stood behind her. When Jessie isn't busy working as an optometrist, he spends time volunteering with the rescue squad. He's the kind of guy who would literally give you the shirt off his back. I'd trust him with my life.

Helen crouched down next to me. "What do you need?"

"We need a backboard. And can you please set up suction in the rig?" I gave the three a brief synopsis of Benjamin's condition. "Who else is with you?"

"Colin Branigan's our driver. Darren Williams is here too. He's driving the other rig." Darren, retired from the army, spends his free time volunteering with our rescue squad.

Benjamin began moaning. Although his eyes stayed closed, he seemed to be gradually waking up. I wanted to see if he could follow simple commands, so I placed my index finger in his hand. "Benjamin, squeeze my finger." *No response.*

Just then, paramedics Ty Fleming and Paula Pritchard arrived. Paula worked many years as a preschool teacher. A few years ago, she decided she wanted a change. She enjoys volunteering as an EMT on her town's first aid squad, so she made the leap and became a paramedic. Ty, who plans one day to be an emergency room physician, is currently taking prerequisite classes to apply for medical school.

"Get him loaded on the backboard," Ty said. "We'll set up in the rig. Did anyone see his car?"

"It's in really bad shape," Sergeant Jamieson said. "Massive damage to the driver's side and a pole landed on top of it too. He was ejected. The train must have pushed the SUV on top of him."

Ty whistled. "Sounds like he's lucky to have gotten this far."

"It sure does. We'll assess him in the rig," Paula said.

We maneuvered Benjamin onto the backboard, strapped him on, lifted him onto the stretcher, and wheeled him toward the ambulance. Just then, our pagers went off.

DISPATCHER: "Second first aid call, one rig on the road. Request for first aid at 614 Chambers Street for a 41-year-old-male fall victim with a right knee injury."

"Since we have two rigs here, Darren and I can cover the knee injury," Helen said. The pair hustled off to respond to the second call.

I spotted Colin sitting in the driver's seat of our ambulance. Jessie, Donna, and I squeezed into the back of the rig with Ty and Paula. Once inside, Ty instructed us to remove Benjamin from the backboard. Then we cut off his clothing to make him "trauma naked." This allows us to make sure we aren't missing anything, such as wounds, bleeding, bruising, open fractures, or other injuries. It also saves precious minutes for the trauma team so they can examine the patient, send him for testing, and possibly even rush him to surgery. Now that his clothes were off, I could see he had a laceration along his right knee and a deep cut along his left heel. I placed a towel over his private parts.

Ty established an intravenous line, and Paula stepped out of the rig to drive their ambulance. "We're all set back here. You can start rolling," Ty instructed Colin.

Jessie took another set of vital signs while I bandaged Benjamin's knee and heel. Perhaps from the pressure of the cuff inflating on his arm, Benjamin opened his eyes.

"Hey there. I'm Ty, a paramedic. We're taking you to the hospital. Can you tell me your name?"

Benjamin looked thoughtful. "Benjamin Wadsworth."

"How old are you?" Ty asked.

"Twenty-nine."

Ty adjusted the flow of the IV line. "Where do you live?"

Benjamin touched the front of his collar with his right hand. "I dunno."

"Can you tell me your date of birth?" Ty asked as he checked Benjamin's blood sugar.

Benjamin nodded and rattled it off. The smell of alcohol emanated from his mouth and pores. It's a good thing you can't get drunk from second-hand alcohol fumes.

"Did you have anything to drink tonight?" Ty asked.

"No."

"Did you take any drugs?"

Benjamin frowned. "No."

Pine Cove is only about ten minutes from the local trauma center. We pulled into the parking garage and prepared to enter the hospital. The trauma team met us at the door, and Ty gave the doctor the patient report. I noticed Sergeant Jamieson had followed us to the hospital in his patrol car. He'd be staying with Benjamin tonight.

We rolled Benjamin into the trauma bay and lifted him from our cot to the hospital stretcher. He sure didn't look like someone who'd just crashed through a barricade, been smashed by a train, had a pole land on top of his SUV, and had his vehicle then land on top of him. All things considered, he didn't look half-bad. As we were leaving, he gave us a crooked smile and a thumbs-up.

As Jessie, Colin, Donna, and I were cleaning our stretcher and putting on fresh linens, Helen and Darren arrived with their patient. We waited until they were done transferring care to the triage nurse, then asked how the man was doing.

"You're not going to believe this," Helen said. "Our patient saw Benjamin hitting his car. When he ran up the driveway to tell his wife, he fell and hurt his knee."

Colin raised his eyebrows. "Geez. Benjamin really knows how to leave a trail of mayhem and destruction."

"We heard he may have hit several other cars too. The police are doing a full investigation," Helen said.

"I wonder how it all came about," I said.

"Me too," Jessie said. "At first, I thought he went around the gates and got hit by the train at the Chambers Street crossing. I figured the train pushed him a block. But then I heard he drove through the barricade at Chestnut Street and got hit there."

"It's going to take some real detective work to get to the bottom of it all," Darren said.

. . . .

One week later, at the squad building following a first aid call

"Has anyone heard how the guy who got hit by the train is doing?" Darren asked.

"I heard he's doing better," Helen said. "I think he has a pelvic fracture. He's supposed to get discharged soon to a rehab facility."

"It's amazing that's all he had," I said as I restocked bandages in the ambulance.

"Jessie, are you done, or do you need help with anything?" Darren asked.

"I just need to check the answering machine for new messages," he replied, pressing the "Play" button.

Our answering machine sprang to life. "Hi, my name is Benjamin Wadsworth. I think you guys took me to the hospital last week. I'm calling because I'm wondering if you have my cell phone."

We didn't. Based on the sheer magnitude of the impact, I'm guessing his cell phone landed in the next state.

God assembled many people on the night of the accident, from police and bystanders to other victims as well as first responders. As dominoes fall in amazing ways, many incidents transpired that night, interweaving to miraculously rescue Benjamin.

Chapter 4

A Tickle in My Throat

A time to weep and a time to laugh,
a time to mourn and a time to dance.

ECCLESIASTES 3:4

DISPATCHER: "Request for first aid at 108 Horizon Avenue for an elderly female fall victim with a possible knee injury."

I shoved the last few articles of clothing—a gray first aid hoodie, a pair of shorts, and my favorite pink socks—from my laundry basket into the washer and turned it on before rushing out the door. When I arrived at the first aid building, I met up with veteran member Archie Harris. Archie, who began volunteering with the rescue squad after a long career with the state government, slid into the driver's seat of our ambulance.

"It looks like it's just you and me for this one," he said.

I clicked the buckle on my seat belt. "We should be fine with the two of us. It sounds straightforward."

Archie nodded and picked up the mic. "We're responding to Horizon Avenue with a light crew. Any additional responding members can meet us at the scene." A "light crew" is code for "we could use some more help."

Two minutes later, we pulled up in front of a light-gray Colonial on an oversized property. Dazzling vincas lined the entry sidewalk, drawing us toward the front door. Archie knocked and called out, "First aid."

A female voice responded, "Come in."

Archie pushed the heavy oak door open, and we found our patient sitting in a high-backed wooden chair in the front foyer. Her faded blue eyes spoke of a lifetime of experiences. Many age spots connected together, making her look like she had a good start on a summer tan. Her short, white wavy hair contrasted with her skin tone, lending her a youthful appearance. She grasped either side of her right knee, guarding and protecting it.

Archie placed our trauma kit close to the woman and introduced us. "Hi. I'm Archie and this is Andrea. We're volunteers with the Pine Cove First Aid Squad. How can we help you this morning?"

Our patient coughed once, then sneezed twice. "I'm Sylvia. Thank you so much for coming. I'm clumsy, and my balance isn't quite what it used to be. About an hour ago, I was vacuuming the living room and tripped on the cord. Wouldn't you know it? I landed right on my right knee, the one with the total knee replacement. At first, I thought it was okay. I figured I could just walk it off. But now it's swelling up like a balloon and feels stiff. I think I better get an X-ray."

I slid the edges of her blue-and-white checkered robe to the sides to expose her knee. I could see bruising over her kneecap and swelling on the inside aspect of her knee. "That's a good idea. We'll take you to the hospital to get checked out. Does it hurt much?"

Sylvia placed her hand over her mouth and coughed several times. "Sorry, I have a tickle in my throat today. I guess it's probably allergies. I was outside quite a bit yesterday. To answer your question, yes, my knee is quite painful."

"Yes, grass pollen gets to me too," Archie said. "We'll put some ice on your knee to help with the pain." We secured Sylvia's knee using a splint with Velcro straps from our "frac pack." I tucked a few cold packs around her knee to help with the swelling and discomfort. She could bear weight on her left leg, so we helped her to pivot using her left leg onto our stretcher. We rolled her out to the ambulance and loaded her inside. After I took her blood pressure and pulse, Archie resumed driving, and we settled down for the trip to the hospital.

I flipped open a notepad and recorded Sylvia's vital signs. "Do you have any medical problems?"

"Just high blood pressure, but I take medication for that." Sylvia coughed. "I'm really quite healthy."

Just then, our ambulance bumped and lurched its way over the train tracks. "Sorry about that. Sometimes the shock absorbers aren't so great on the ambulances."

Sylvia sneezed. "I'm just glad you could help me."

I handed her a tissue. I hoped her coughing and sneezing were indeed due to allergies and not a cold or other illness. I'm too busy to get sick.

Soon, we arrived at the hospital, transferred her care to the emergency department staff, and said our goodbyes. I patted her arm. "Hopefully, it's just a bruise and you'll be home again before you know it."

As Archie and I exited the ED, our pagers began beeping. It seemed as if we wouldn't be getting home anytime soon.

DISPATCHER: "Request for first aid at 112 Horizon Avenue for a fall victim."

As soon as we got in the ambulance, Archie called us in service. "Please have any additional members meet us at the scene."

"This call is just two doors down from the last one. What a strange coincidence," I said.

"Yes, and both falls. Let's hope it's nothing serious."

Archie stopped at a red light until traffic came to a halt and allowed him to proceed through. Within a few minutes, we arrived at our call location: a small white Cape Cod with an attached single-car garage. As we pulled up, I spotted members Clint Edwards and Colleen Harper arriving in their personal vehicles. Colleen joined years ago as a cadet and now is in school to become a speech-language pathologist.

"Sorry I missed the last one. I just got home from the grocery store," Colleen said.

I followed her into the home and found Officer Jack Endicott and Sergeant Derrick Flint providing care to a slim, elderly gentleman who'd taken a spill, landing face first in a potted plant. At a glance, it looked like the plant won. The man's nose appeared swollen, bruised, and a bit crooked, indicating a possible fracture. Blood trickled from a small laceration on the bridge of his nose and out of his left nostril.

"My name's Harvey," the man said gruffly. "I'm so embarrassed. I can't believe I fell and dragged all you people over here on such a nice day."

"It's okay. That's what we're here for," I said. Accidents, including fall victims, are one of our most common types of calls.

"He's on a blood thinner," Sergeant Flint noted.

When older folks on blood thinners fall and strike their heads, they're at a higher risk for brain bleeds. We always recommend transport to the emergency room. The emergency room physician may opt to do a CT scan to evaluate for head injury.

I knelt next to Harvey and slid my fingers onto the thumb side of his left wrist to check his pulse. Suddenly, I had a tremendous urge to cough—the kind of cough in which you try so desperately to hold it in that your eyes start watering. My attempts to hold the cough in weren't working very well, and I feared I might unleash a torrent of coughing, which is not what I would consider good form while you're right in your patient's face. So I abandoned my attempt to finish taking Harvey's pulse, stood up, and hurried outside.

My mind raced. *I don't get it. I wasn't sick when I woke up this morning. How could I come down with something this fast?* Was Sylvia, the patient from earlier this morning, actually sick rather than suffering from allergies? But even if she was ill, there's no way I could have caught it from her and started showing symptoms myself this quickly. I walked far enough away from the front door that I wouldn't appear conspicuous. Then I surrendered wholeheartedly to my insatiable desire to cough. However, coughing didn't make the urge subside. Instead, it seemed to inflame it. I kept hacking.

A minute later, Clint joined me outside. "Where'd you go?"

I paused coughing long enough to reply. "I'm sorry. I would have told you, but I couldn't really speak because I had to cough, and I didn't want to do it in there."

I looked at him more closely. His face was red, and his eyes began watering. "I came out for the same reason," he said. "All of a sudden, I had a tremendous urge to cough. I tried, but I just can't hold it in." Then he began coughing too!

We looked at each other. *What in the world is going on?*

"Something in there must have irritated our throats, but I didn't notice anything out of the ordinary," I said.

"Me neither."

Just then, Sergeant Flint and Officer Endicott stepped outside, joining us on the front walk. I noticed Officer Endicott stifling a cough as he strode past us toward the curb and watched as he placed something near the edge of the road.

"We both can't stop coughing. Is there something wrong in there?" I asked.

Sergeant Flint cleared his throat. "Jack just realized his mace has a slow leak. There's no way to stop it, so he's putting it far away until it's empty."

No wonder I had a tickle in my throat! Now, it all made sense. Fortunately, Harvey didn't react to the mace. Clint's and my coughing subsided enough that we could transport him to the emergency room without incident.

As volunteers, we often must come to terms with witnessing sadness, heartache, and death. On this call, we were able to witness the lighter side of answering first aid calls. After exiting the emergency department, we had a good laugh about our sudden "illness."

Chapter 5

The Mysterious Chest Wound

"Be strong and courageous.
Do not be afraid; do not be discouraged,
for the LORD your God will be with you wherever you go."

JOSHUA 1:9

A mother never stops worrying about her children. Even though Danielle Stueben was in her early seventies, she still fretted about her daughter Gilda. She knew Gilda worked her waitressing job last night, and now she wanted to make sure she was safe and sound. Danielle's husband had died from pancreatic cancer about ten years ago. Gilda got a divorce from her husband at about the same time. Danielle was happy when Gilda moved in with her because she liked the company. It also helped to refocus some of the grief she felt at the loss of her long-time spouse.

Danielle had heard Gilda come in just past one o'clock in the morning. She'd been loud when she first entered, but now the house seemed unusually quiet. She was surprised Gilda appeared to have fallen asleep so quickly. Usually, she could hear her shoes clunking onto the floor and her creaky closet door opening and closing. She decided to peek into her daughter's room and make sure everything was okay.

The door to Gilda's room stood partly open, so Danielle gave it a firm nudge. Blackness enveloped the room, and Danielle paused at the threshold as her eyes adjusted to the darkness. She noticed Gilda seemed flung across the bed at an odd angle, not neatly tucked in like usual.

"Gilda?" she whispered. No response.

Danielle's gut told her something was wrong. She gently shook her daughter's shoulder. Gilda moaned softly. Danielle flipped on the light and saw…blood. Copious blood. Everywhere. The floor, the blankets, and all over Gilda. *How? Why?* She stifled a scream.

Danielle backpedaled out of the room, grabbing onto the doorframe to steady herself. *Phone, find a phone.* She feared if she didn't get help quickly, her daughter could bleed to death. She located her cordless phone downstairs in the kitchen and shakily dialed 911. "I need an ambulance for my daughter…"

. . . .

DISPATCHER: "Request for first aid at 1219 Sunset Drive for abdominal bleeding."

Groggily, I sat up in bed and began pulling on a pair of sweatpants that I keep on a nearby chair. *Abdominal bleeding. Maybe a rectal bleed?* Lower gastrointestinal bleeds are a common type of first aid call. As I slipped on a pair of shoes, my pager beeped again.

DISPATCHER: "Update for first aid call at 1219 Sunset Drive. The nature is for an abdominal laceration."

How did a person sustain a wound to their abdomen at one o'clock in the morning? Was it self-inflicted? Or did someone injure the person? Was a knife or gun involved? Or perhaps the person had a recent abdominal surgery, and now the incision was reopening. Questions swirled in my head, helping me mentally prepare for whatever I might find.

I grabbed my keys off the small hook by the back door and jumped into my car. Soon, I was rushing toward the first aid building. I planned to pass Sunset Drive and continue toward our headquarters, but just as I approached the vicinity of the call, Jessie Barnes called the ambulance in service. So instead of proceeding to the building, I made a quick left onto Sunset. Inky blackness covered the quiet side street until I grew closer to the 1200 block. Then, the flashing lights of two patrol cars illuminated the darkness. I parked and hurried down a long asphalt driveway followed by a lengthy concrete walkway. When I reached the front door, I found it propped open. I stepped inside, uncertain of what our patient's condition would be.

I didn't have to wait long to find out, for soon after I entered, I spotted a partially clad woman who looked to be in her mid-thirties seated in a wooden chair, just past the kitchen and close to the entrance to the dining room. Her long dark hair partially obscured her face. My eyes swept downward, and I took a quick deep breath at the extraordinary amount of blood. Puddles of red soaked the hallway. As I stepped closer, I could see splashes of blood on the walls as well. Bright-red blood covered the woman from her neck to the tips of her toes.

Officer Brad Sims pressed sterile combine dressings securely on the woman's chest in an effort to control the bleeding. A formidable six foot three, Officer Sims looks as if he'd be as comfortable playing on a football field as he does in his police uniform. I realized this call was probably dispatched as an abdominal wound rather than a chest wound because there was so much blood, it was difficult for the 911 caller to identify where the blood originated from.

"Sergeant Flint is upstairs investigating," Sims said. "This is Gilda Stueben. Her mother, Danielle, found her in bed bleeding profusely and called 911 right away. Gilda was initially unconscious but came around when her mother called her name and shook her shoulder. Danielle said Gilda seemed unaware that she was bleeding. She stood up and staggered out of the bedroom and downstairs. She collapsed here in this chair and passed out again for about a minute. When we arrived, she was semiconscious."

A young officer from Sandy Springs, a nearby town, stood just to the left of Officer Sims. He must have heard the call on his police radio and came over to offer assistance. The local police departments work well together, supporting each other during times of need.

Blood began seeping through the multiple dressings already applied to Gilda's chest. *Could this be a life-threatening laceration?* I reached into the police officers' first aid bag and grabbed another combine dressing. I tore it open and handed it to Sims, who added it to the stack on Gilda's chest. If a wound is bleeding, it's important not to "peek" and pull back the dressings, as this can rip away any fragile clots that may be forming.

"Did you get a look at the wound before you applied the dressings?" I asked.

Sims nodded. "It's a deep laceration on the right side of the chest. It was spurting when we got here."

"Do you think it's a sucking chest wound?" This is an extremely dangerous condition in which there is a hole in the chest wall. Air collects outside the lung and can cause it to collapse, otherwise known as pneumothorax. These types of injuries are typically caused by stabbings, gunshot wounds, or impalement. When the person breathes in, it creates a sucking noise (hence the name) because air travels directly into the chest cavity via the hole. It's a life-threatening injury requiring rapid treatment and transport. The key is to prevent air from entering the chest via the wound, while at the same time allowing air that's already in the chest cavity to escape. In the field, we use an occlusive dressing, which we can "burp" to let air out.

"It's hard to tell with all the blood, but I don't think so. She doesn't appear to be in respiratory distress." Signs of a sucking chest include chest pain, difficulty breathing, rapid heart rate and breathing, bleeding from the wound, and a sucking noise with respiration. Although Gilda had severe bleeding from the wound and an increased heart rate, she didn't appear to have the other signs.

Gilda's face was stark white, possibly a sign of hemorrhagic shock. With this condition, a person loses so much blood that they can no longer meet their tissues' requirements for oxygen.

"Has she spoken to you at all?" I asked.

Sims shook his head. "Not yet. She's been pretty out of it."

"Could it be a gunshot wound?" *Had Gilda shot herself in an attempt to take her own life? Had someone else shot her?* "Let's lean her forward and check for an exit wound."

Careful to maintain strong pressure over her wound, we leaned her forward and studied her entire back, from the nape of her neck to her tailbone. I didn't spot anything resembling an exit wound. Of course, that didn't mean it wasn't a gunshot wound, for the bullet could have been lodged somewhere within her chest.

Sims helped me lean Gilda back again. Her eyes popped open, and she went from semiconscious to alert and wide awake in the span of just a few seconds. Confusion as to why strangers were leaning over her blossomed into fear as she realized blood soaked her. She caught sight of her mother standing behind me.

"Mom, what's happening?"

She began to tremble. The Sandy Springs officer draped a large towel around her shoulders.

Mrs. Stueben looked as if she was one pager alert shy of becoming a first aid call herself. "Gilda, we don't know. I thought you could tell us what happened. Why are you bleeding?" Her voice caught on the word bleeding, and she seemed to somehow finish the sentence using sheer willpower.

"Gilda, it's very important we find out what happened to you. Did you get in a fight with someone before you came home?" Sims asked.

Gilda gasped. "Was I in a fight? Have I been shot? Did someone shoot me?"

"How did you get home tonight?" Sims asked. "Did you drive?"

Gilda waited a few seconds to reply. "I took a cab. Do you think the driver shot me?" She glanced down at her chest. "Did he stab me?"

"We're going to figure all that out," Sims said. He turned toward me. "If you want to take over, I'll go outside and do some investigating. I saw quite a bit of blood out on the driveway on my way in. When we got here, our first concern was to help her. Now that you're here, I want to figure out what happened."

"I've got this," I said. "You go ahead."

Gilda's non-rebreather oxygen mask slipped slightly. Keeping firm pressure on her chest with one hand, I quickly tightened the strap with my other. Blood continued to seep through the additional dressing, and I resumed holding pressure with both hands.

I turned toward the Sandy Springs police officer. "I think the ambulance just arrived. Can you please ask them to bring in a bulky trauma dressing?"

Sergeant Flint came downstairs holding a blood-soaked striped top. "There's a small hole in the chest area of the shirt she was wearing when she got home."

"A hole in my shirt?" Gilda said. "Did someone shoot me?"

"The police are working on figuring out what happened," I said, hoping to soothe her.

Fellow volunteer EMT squad members Archie Harris, Ted O'Malley, Donna Ferlise, and Jessie Barnes entered the room. Archie handed me a trauma dressing, and I placed it over the combine dressings. Fortunately, the bleeding appeared to be slowing down a bit. Donna took one look at Gilda's mother and immediately assisted her to a nearby chair in the kitchen.

I quickly filled them in on what we knew so far.

"The medics pulled in right behind us, so they should be coming in any second," Ted said as he began to check Gilda's blood pressure. "Her blood pressure is 108 over 72."

Gilda grabbed hold of my forearm and squeezed tightly. "Am I going to die? Am I going to bleed to death?"

"No, the bleeding is slowing down." So far, the blood hadn't seeped through the trauma dressing. The direct pressure was working, helping to stem the flow of blood.

Paramedics Rose Anderson and William Moore arrived and placed their equipment on the floor next to Gilda.

"I think someone may have shot me, but I can't remember," Gilda said.

I wondered how much alcohol she'd had tonight and if it was

impairing her memory of the events leading up to and including her injury.

"How about a hemostatic dressing?" Archie suggested, holding one up with his right hand.

"No, we'll hold off on that. Let's get her onto the stair chair and into the rig," William said. Due to several tight corners, we couldn't bring the stretcher close enough to Gilda. Because she couldn't walk, we would need the stair chair to maneuver her safely out of the house.

Sergeant Flint and Officer Sims rejoined us in the kitchen. "Gilda, are you sure you took a cab home?"

Gilda bit her lip. "Yes. No. I'm not sure. I thought I did."

It would make sense that she took a cab home if she'd been drinking. It also made sense that she might not want to admit she drove home even if she did, for it could be construed as driving while intoxicated. Not exactly something you'd want to advertise to police officers.

Now that the bleeding had slowed, we wrapped Kling wrap around Gilda's thorax to hold the dressing in place. "Stand up with me," Archie instructed, pivoting her from the chair to the stair chair.

We rolled the chair outside to the sidewalk, where Jessie had set up the stretcher. After assisting her onto the stretcher, Archie and Ted rolled her to the ambulance. Jessie resumed the driver's seat and Ted sat next to him to act as his copilot. Rose drove the medic rig, and the rest of us climbed into the back of the ambulance. I sat in the small side seat next to Gilda and Archie and William sat on the bench across from me. Donna sat in the captain's chair and began documenting the call information.

"Do you remember anything about tonight?" William asked.

Gilda's intoxication seemed to be wearing off. "Well, I remember going to work."

"Where's that?" William prodded her as he prepared an intravenous line.

"I'm a waitress at a Mexican restaurant about five miles from here," she replied. "Do you think someone there stabbed me?"

"The police are figuring out what happened," I said, slipping a pulse ox onto her middle finger.

"What did you do after work? Did you go out somewhere? Maybe for a drink?" William asked.

Gilda scratched her head with her right hand, now caked with dried blood. "Well, yes, I think so. I think I went to a bar for a few drinks on the way home."

My guess was more than a few drinks. She'd seemed quite inebriated when we first arrived. Now, the circumstances were effectively killing whatever buzz she had left.

"Maybe I took a cab home. Maybe the driver attacked me," Gilda said.

"Well, we'll find out soon enough," William said. "Right now, we're going to bring you into a trauma room in the emergency department so they can check this wound more closely. Have you ever thought about harming yourself?"

Gilda shook her head vehemently. "I don't want to die. I wouldn't do this to myself."

Her vital signs remained stable, and she continued to breathe adequately.

"I can't believe the wound is on my chest. My heart is there."

"Well, the injury is on the right side of your chest and your heart is on the left," I said, hoping to reassure her and decrease some of her anxiety.

Gilda blinked a few times in rapid succession. "Oh, well that's something, I guess."

Once we arrived at the hospital, we took her into a trauma bay, and William gave the report to the trauma doc. I hoped we'd be able to learn their findings. Once we leave someone at the hospital, we often never get to find out what was wrong.

After we climbed back into the ambulance, Jessie told the dispatcher our rig was back in service. "I wonder if the police figured out exactly what happened yet."

"I'd love to know what caused that wound," Donna said, sliding a fresh pillowcase onto one of our pillows. "I can't imagine a cab driver attacking her."

"Me neither. And she seemed sincere when she claimed she wasn't trying to harm herself," I said.

"And it didn't seem like a gunshot wound," Archie said.

"The case of the mysterious chest wound," Donna quipped.

A few days later, we learned that Gilda had an alcohol flask in her right inner coat pocket. She must have tripped on her driveway, with the subsequent impact shattering the bottle and causing her chest laceration. Since she'd been drinking, she forgot she fell and didn't realize anything was wrong until she spotted the blood.

I reflected it was truly a blessing Gilda somehow was able to get up and inside so that her mother could assist her. Otherwise, it's possible she could have bled to death.

Chapter 6

Ain't Misbehaving

Be kind and compassionate to one another,
forgiving each other,
just as in Christ God forgave you.
EPHESIANS 4:32

After jogging with my kids, I enjoyed a beautiful late spring evening by walking our dogs with my husband, Rick. We were a block and a half from home when my pager began beeping.

DISPATCHER: "Request for first aid for a female, unresponsive but breathing. Patient is on the west side of the train station."

I ran track in grammar and high school but haven't run consistently in years. I'm definitely more of a walker than a jogger at this point in my life. My quads were already burning in protest from my earlier run. Nevertheless, I picked up our 13-pound Shih Tzu rescue, Scooby, and began jogging home. My legs threatened to rebel, but I kept (sort of) running.

DISPATCHER: "Update: patient is in the second car of the train."

After reaching home, I deposited Scooby safely indoors, grabbed my car keys (yes, I admit to heavy breathing at this point, but vigorously deny gasping for air), and headed for the Pine Cove train station. On the way, I couldn't help but ponder what may have caused our patient's problem. *A heart attack? Stroke? Seizure? Intoxication?* Was she alone or with someone who could provide us with pertinent background information? Sometimes, being an EMT involves detective work. It's one of the things I enjoy most about my volunteer work with the rescue squad.

As I arrived, the train was just pulling into the station. The conductor must have called 911 while the train was still traveling southward, requesting EMS meet them at the next scheduled stop. The long train blocked me from driving across the tracks to the first aid building to meet the ambulance, so I parked at the train station instead. I knew the ambulance would meet me at the scene.

I followed Officer Jack Endicott and three other Pine Cove police officers onto the second car of the train. Our town doesn't have an elevated platform, so it's several big steps to climb aboard. The commuter train was crowded with passengers eager to go home after a long day in the city. Several curious faces stared at us, interested in observing the medical emergency unfolding before them. A few others seemed impatient that the first aid call could cause a delay, while others appeared disinterested.

Late afternoon sunlight filtered through tinted windows. The odor of antiseptic mixed with that hard-to-exactly-describe "train smell" hung in the air. Midway down the train car, one of our members, Jocelyn Farnsworth, squatted near the victim. Jocelyn owns a local bakery. When she isn't creating delicious desserts, she volunteers with our squad.

Our patient was bent all the way forward, so I couldn't see her face. I squeezed past her to her other side, closer to the train window. I supported her head and shoulders while Jocelyn swung her legs onto the train bench, such that she was now lying on her back. I opened her airway by tilting her head back and lifting her chin. In this way, we could make sure her tongue wasn't blocking her airway. Officer Endicott flipped the seat back of the bench in front of us in the other direction so we'd have more room to work.

Our victim, a middle-aged woman, wore torn jeans and a faded, stained green T-shirt. Gray-streaked brown hair fell across her face, so I swept it out of the way with a gloved hand. She remained unconscious with agonal (gasping) breaths. Her face had an unnatural bluish hue with underlying pale splotchiness. She clearly wasn't getting enough oxygen. Without immediate medical intervention, I feared she could soon transition into cardiac arrest.

Officer Endicott passed me a non-rebreather mask hooked to a portable oxygen tank. "You can put this on her while I set up the BVM," he said. I slid the mask onto her face, pinching the metal clasp at the bridge of her nose and tightening the elastic straps that went around her head.

An unkempt woman alone on a train, not responding and barely breathing. What could be the source of her sudden illness? I recalled the opioid overdose triad: decreased level of responsiveness (yes), depressed respiratory effort (definitely yes), and pinpoint pupils. I gently pulled the woman's left eyelid upwards. *Bingo. Pinpoint pupils. Time for naloxone.*

Naloxone, an opioid antagonist, is the generic name for Narcan. It's the antidote to an opioid overdose. It displaces the opioid from the opioid receptor in the nervous system. Opioids include drugs like heroin, fentanyl, and oxycodone. If naloxone is administered in time, it will completely reverse the effects of an opioid overdose. In the field, police and EMS most commonly administer it through a person's nasal passages. Naloxone won't help if the person overdosed on something other than an opioid. It also won't be of benefit if the person has been without a pulse (i.e., in cardiac arrest) for too long.

Officer Endicott pulled naloxone from his jump kit. I temporarily pulled the non-rebreather mask out of the way so he could insert the medication into the woman's left nostril. If we were correct in our assessment, she should start improving within a few minutes. In the meantime, we had to make sure she had adequate oxygenation.

Squad members Colin Branigan and Buddy Stone arrived with our equipment. Buddy, a retired pharmaceuticals salesman, helped our squad when he wasn't busy babysitting his grandchildren.

Colin had just gotten off from his shift working as a chef. He leaned over the train seatback. "What do you need?"

"Can you set up the defibrillator, just in case we need it?" I asked.

Colin nodded. "You got it." He turned away to prepare the SAED for possible use.

Jocelyn placed two fingers along the radial side of the woman's wrist. "I can't feel a radial pulse, but her carotid is 40."

In EMS, we use the 80/70/60 rule. If you can feel a person's radial pulse, that means the systolic (top number) of the blood pressure is at least 80 mmHg. If you feel the femoral pulse at the groin, the systolic blood pressure is at least 70 mmHg. Palpating a carotid pulse at the neck means the person has a systolic blood pressure of 60mmHG or greater. Since Jocelyn couldn't feel a radial pulse, that meant the top number of this woman's blood pressure was less than 80 mmHg. Not good.

Officer Endicott handed me the BVM. "We just got an ID. Her name is Saralee Kesler."

I replaced the non-rebreather with the BVM and began rescue breathing at a rate of one breath every five seconds. So far, the naloxone hadn't improved her condition.

Jocelyn placed a blood-pressure cuff around Saralee's upper arm, pumped it up, and listened closely with her stethoscope. "I can't hear a pressure, but it's only 60 by palpation." Normal blood pressure is 120/80. If we can't hear (auscultate) blood pressure with a stethoscope, we can obtain a systolic (top number) only by inflating the cuff and feeling for a pulse. This method is called obtaining a blood pressure "by palpation." Saralee's blood pressure was dangerously low.

Officer Endicott pulled a second dose of naloxone from the kit. "The medics are about five minutes out."

I heard the sound of muffled crying. I glanced up between administering rescue breaths and spotted two women across the aisle, obviously deeply affected by our patient's plight. Hands clasped; they began fervently praying.

Saralee's condition hadn't improved despite receiving the naloxone.

"It's time for another dose," I said.

Officer Endicott handed it to me, and I inserted it into Saralee's right nostril. Although the blue hue of her face changed to a pale pink, she remained unresponsive.

"I have the stretcher set up by the train door. I brought in the scoop, but I don't think it's going to work," Buddy said. The scoop is a rigid stretcher that splits into two pieces. It's very useful for "scooping" patients up. But the way Saralee was wedged in the tight quarters of the train seat, it could prove extremely difficult to utilize in this situation.

"Her blood pressure's coming up a bit. It's 66 over 40 now," Jocelyn said.

Saralee's respiratory effort improved, and she began breathing on her own. *The naloxone is working.* I switched from the BVM back to the non-rebreather mask.

Officer Endicott stepped in closer. "She's not very big. I'll carry her out." I supported Saralee's head and Colin lifted her waist as Officer Endicott lifted her up into his arms. He began working his way down the aisle toward the exit. I followed behind holding the oxygen tank. I noticed the two women across the aisle continued to bow their heads in prayer. They looked up as we passed, tears sliding down their cheeks. Their prayers were working.

Further down the train car, I noticed several other women with misty eyes, shaken up by the sight. As EMS volunteers, we're used to seeing sad, horrible, and even gruesome occurrences. But for most people, like the passengers on this train, it's traumatic to see a middle-aged woman collapse in such a manner.

Officer Endicott placed Saralee gently on the cot. Just as he did, she opened her eyes. At first, she had that what-in-the-world-happened-and-who-are-you-people look on her face. We rolled her into the ambulance, and Jocelyn, Colin, and I climbed in the back with her. Buddy returned to the driver's seat, ready to take us to the hospital.

While the rear doors were still open, Officer Endicott passed me Saralee's pocketbook. "We were able to make contact with a friend of hers. She has a history of stroke and seizures. She takes an anticonvulsant, but her friend isn't sure of the name of it," he said.

Jocelyn switched the oxygen from the portable tank to the onboard unit. "Can you tell us your name?"

After a short pause, as if trying to recall her name, she said, "Saralee."

"And where do you live?" Jocelyn continued.

"In the city," Saralee responded vaguely. "I'm on my way to see my father."

That didn't add up. The train was going away from the city, not toward it.

"Were you alone on the train?" I asked.

Saralee looked thoughtful. "I don't know, but I ain't been misbehaving."

She must know passengers who "misbehave" get removed from the train at the next stop. Her reply seemed almost automatic, as if perhaps she'd been escorted off the train in the past.

"Your friend Gary got off several stops ago. We're trying to track him down," Officer Endicott said before shutting the door.

"The medics can meet us on the way. We'll rendezvous with them at the ballfield parking lot," Buddy called back to us from the driver's seat. He picked up the mic to speak to the dispatcher. "We're enroute to Bakersville Hospital, meeting up with the medics on the way."

I pushed Saralee's sleeve up to get another blood pressure reading. "What did you take on the train?"

Saralee closed her eyes for a minute before responding. "Heroin."

I wrapped the automatic cuff around her arm. "How much?"

"Two bags."

"How much do you usually take?"

"Two bags, but Gary got it from a different dealer," she said.

"Did you snort it?" I asked.

Saralee pulled at her left eyebrow. "Yeah."

I wondered if the heroin was cut with fentanyl. That could explain her severe reaction. "Blood pressure is going up a bit. Now it's 100 over 60."

Buddy pulled into the ballfield parking lot and a pair of medics I didn't know climbed in. After a brief assessment, they released Saralee to our care. I was surprised, given the initial severity of her overdose. Opioids such as fentanyl, heroin, and methadone have a longer half-life than naloxone. That means patients must be monitored carefully because the helpful effect of the naloxone can wear off and the patient can relapse. That is, symptoms such as respiratory depression can reoccur.

As we pulled into the emergency department parking lot, Saralee became less responsive. She could still say her name, but she could no longer answer other questions.

I patted Saralee's shoulder. "Stay awake. We're at the hospital."

Saralee nodded, but her eyes remained closed.

Once Buddy parked, Colin opened the rear doors and began pulling out the stretcher. "Let's get her in fast. She looks like she may need more naloxone."

Nurse Maggie Summers met us at the triage desk. After we filled her in on Saralee's condition, she paged for a doctor to come to the triage area stat.

Dr. Morgan arrived promptly. "Let's get an IV in her, and we'll give her more naloxone," he said.

Maggie established an intravenous line, and Dr. Morgan injected the naloxone. Within a minute, Saralee began waking up again. By the time we moved her from our stretcher to the hospital's, she could speak.

Saralee's guardian angel must have been watching over her that day. She was extremely fortunate that she overdosed on a train and another passenger noticed she collapsed. If she'd overdosed alone at home, she would surely have passed away that day. Now, through the grace of God and the kindness and prayers of strangers, she has a chance to change her life and walk away from illicit narcotics.

Chapter 7

More Time Together

*"Consecrate yourselves, for tomorrow the Lord
will do amazing things among you."*
JOSHUA 3:5

Brett Hincks slowly opened his eyes, blinked a few times, and rolled to his right side to check the time on his digital alarm clock. *2:17 a.m.* He returned to his back and stared up at the ceiling. A nightlight cast a small amount of light, just enough to relieve the stark darkness. His wife, Roselyn, doted on him like a mother hen. In fact, so did his daughter, Jasmine. They were both passionate about home safety and preventing falls. A few years ago, he tripped on the way to the bathroom and broke a couple ribs. They installed nightlights in the bedroom and bathroom the very next day.

Now, Brett felt that something seemed wrong, but he couldn't put a finger on it. He figured the hot air from the heating system had dried out his nasal passages and throat. He reasoned that a cup of water might help him go back to sleep.

Brett tossed his legs off the edge of the bed and slipped his feet into a pair of cozy fleece-lined moccasin slippers. When he stood up, a wave of dizziness washed over him. He recalled his doctor telling him not to get up too fast or his blood pressure might suddenly drop. He paused a moment, then took a few steps toward the bathroom, hoping the light-headedness would pass.

. . . .

Jasmine Hincks awoke with a start to a loud thump. She realized the noise had come from her parents' bedroom and prayed her father hadn't taken another tumble. She'd moved back home about two years ago to help out after her mother was diagnosed with breast cancer. Her mom suffered through over a month of daily radiation therapy and numerous rounds of chemotherapy that made her hair fall out and her hands and feet tingle from neuropathy. Now, things were looking decidedly brighter. Her mother's latest mammogram showed no signs of recurrent cancer. The family embraced the magical words "cancer free."

Jasmine flipped on the overhead lights as she entered her parents' bedroom. Her father was sprawled awkwardly on the floor on his right side. She rushed to him and knelt down next to him. "Dad, what's wrong? What happened?"

Brett frowned. "I'm not sure. I got up to get a drink of water. The next thing I know, I'm on the ground. I guess I fell."

"Are you okay? Are you hurt?" Jasmine grabbed a pillow from Brett's side of the king-sized bed and placed it under his head.

"I'm not hurt. Just my pride. I just need to get up, and I'm sure I'll be fine."

Roselyn slept through Brett's fall but now awoke from the commotion. "What's going on?" she asked sleepily.

"Dad fell, but he's okay," Jasmine replied. "I'm going to try to help him up."

"Oh, no!" Now fully alert, Roselyn sprang out of bed to assist.

Brett shifted onto his back. "I remember feeling dizzy when I stood up. I wonder if I passed out."

Jasmine frowned. "Do you still feel dizzy? I can check your blood pressure before we try to get you up."

"Not dizzy, exactly. But not great, either. I can't really pinpoint it. I just don't feel that good. Not like my usual self."

"Honey, is the room spinning? Like the time you had vertigo?" Roselyn asked.

"No, it feels different than that. But I can't describe it. It's like a funny flutter in my chest."

Jasmine slipped her fingers onto Brett's wrist. "Your pulse feels fast. And your face looks sweaty."

Brett touched his left ear. "I know I don't hear very well, but there's a rushing noise in my ears. What do you think that means?"

Roselyn paced back and forth, uncertain what to do. "I'm not sure what that could be from, honey."

Jasmine rose to her feet. "I'll be right back. I think the blood-pressure cuff is in the kitchen." She rushed downstairs and located an automatic blood-pressure machine on the granite counter near the toaster oven. She grabbed it and raced back upstairs. When she reentered the bedroom, Roselyn was kneeling over Brett.

Roselyn tried to contain her rising panic. "Honey, I think something's wrong. His eyes rolled back in his head, and now he's not answering me."

Jasmine knelt next to Brett and shook his shoulder. She noticed that he looked unnaturally pale, as if all the blood had drained from his head. "Dad, wake up."

No response.

She shook him harder, trying to quell her rising fear. "Dad!"

Hands shaking, Roselyn picked up the cordless telephone on Brett's night table. "I'm calling 911."

. . . .

DISPATCHER: "Request for first aid at 816 Sawyer Street for an 83-year-old male, unconscious, unknown if breathing."

Long-time Pine Cove First Aid Squad volunteer Buddy Stone slid into the ambulance's driver's seat and keyed the mic. "On the ramp, awaiting a crew."

"Received. Be advised I'm going to redispatch the call," dispatcher Jerome Franklin replied.

DISPATCHER: "Request for first aid at 816 Sawyer Street for an 83-year-old male. Expedite. CPR in progress by a family member. Patrols are tied up on a different call."

"I have members arriving," Buddy said. "We'll be in service to Sawyer Street." As soon as Ted O'Malley, Archie Harris, and I climbed into the ambulance, Buddy flipped on the overhead emergency lights. Few other vehicles were on the road. I supposed most people were safely tucked into their beds for the night. Buddy stopped briefly at a red light. Since no other cars were coming, he proceeded through the intersection.

Ted shifted from the captain's chair to the rig's bench, pulling equipment from one of the cabinets while he was on his feet. "I've got the defibrillator and suction."

Archie donned a pair of medical gloves. "I've got the oxygen, airways, and BVM ready to go."

I jotted the dispatch time and location at the top of our run sheet. "I recognize this address. I think the Hincks live here. I used to work with Jasmine Hincks years ago. This could be her father."

"I think you're right. I know the Hincks too. I guess we're about to find out for sure," Archie said.

"We're on location," Buddy notified dispatch.

Time is of the essence during a cardiac arrest, as precious brain cells can be permanently damaged if a person doesn't receive an adequate supply of oxygen. In fact, brain cells can begin dying less than five minutes after the oxygen supply disappears.

A flustered-looking older woman wearing a white robe and beige slippers stood on the front porch, holding the door wide open for us. "Archie, is that you? I'm so glad you're here. Brett is upstairs. I don't think he's breathing." She led us through the front foyer and up a dimly lit flight of carpeted stairs to a large bedroom.

Jasmine looked up as we entered. Although it's been years since we worked together, she recognized me right away.

"Andrea, this is my father. I've been doing CPR as best I can, but it's been a long time since I've been certified." She stood up and moved a few steps back to give us room to work.

"Can you tell us exactly what happened today?" Buddy asked as he ripped open a package of defibrillator electrode pads.

Jasmine took a deep breath, trying to stay calm. "Dad went to get a drink of water. I woke up when I heard him fall. He said he felt dizzy and had a flutter in his chest. Then he passed out and stopped breathing."

Archie knelt next to Brett's chest and placed his fingers on his carotid artery. "No pulse. Continue CPR." He began pressing on Brett's chest, counting softly out loud with each compression. "One, and two, and three, and four…"

I knelt at Brett's head. His face appeared paler than a bucket of white paint, his lips punctuating the pallor with a dash of bluish-purple. Lifeless eyes stared unseeing. Brett was no longer with us. Instead, his soul hovered somewhere between Earth and the eternal afterlife. I couldn't imagine the pain and fear that Jasmine and Roselyn must be feeling right now. I tilted Brett's head back and lifted his chin to open his airway, then placed the mask of the BVM over his nose and mouth. I began administering ventilations at a rate of two breaths for every 15 compressions.

Buddy applied the electrode pads to Brett's chest and turned on the semiautomatic external defibrillator (SAED). "Everybody clear," he said, pressing the unit's analyze button.

Jasmine clasped Roselyn's hand and pulled her close. Together, they began softly praying. The machine made a whirring noise as it created a charge. "Shock advised," it announced.

"Stand clear," Buddy repeated and pressed the shock button. The defibrillator sent a dose of electric current to the heart, depolarizing it in an attempt to correct Brett's abnormal heart rhythm and restore his circulation.

Archie placed two fingers along the side of Brett's neck. "Hey, I feel a pulse. Continue with ventilations. I'll get a blood pressure." He applied a cuff to Brett's upper arm. "His blood pressure is 90 over 50, and his pulse is 80 and irregular."

"The paramedics are about five minutes out," Buddy noted. "We can get Brett on a backboard and meet them in the ambulance."

Roselyn fought back tears. "Do you think he's going to be okay?"

"We're doing everything we possibly can," Ted said. "We're going to meet the paramedics downstairs. They can give your husband advanced life support, like medications for his heart. Right now, he has a pulse, but we're helping him to breathe." His words were designed to be honest yet give much-needed hope.

Together, we carefully rolled Brett onto a backboard and strapped him in. By the time we carried him downstairs, veteran paramedic team Kennisha Smythe and Arthur Williamson arrived.

"Since you have him already packaged, we'll set up in the rig. One of you can come with us and give the report," Kennisha said.

"I can," I offered.

Jasmine turned to her mother and squeezed her tightly. "Grab what you need, and I'll drive us to the hospital. We can meet Dad there."

My heart went out to both. I could tell Jasmine was trying to stay strong for her mother's sake. I followed the medics to the rig and explained the course of events: Brett's collapse, his daughter starting CPR, and regaining a pulse after one shock with the defibrillator.

On the way to the hospital, Brett's condition didn't improve, but it didn't deteriorate either. Uncertain of what his future might hold, I clung to the hope that for at least now, he was alive.

. . . .

Three weeks later

Much to my delight, I ran into Jasmine at the grocery store. "How's your dad?"

"Dad's making an absolutely remarkable recovery. After the ER doctors stabilized him, they brought him straight to the cardiac cath lab. The cardiologist said he cleaned out a blockage and put in a stent to make sure it'll stay open. He also gave Dad a combination pacemaker and internal defibrillator. That way, if his heart ever stops again, the defibrillator will automatically shock him. I can't get over how terrific he's doing."

I beamed. "What wonderful news!"

Life is so fragile. Now, the Hincks family had an opportunity to spend more time together on Earth. A true gift.

Jasmine smiled in return. "I can't thank all of you enough. When I think back to that night, it's truly a miracle he's still alive."

P.S. Brett and Roselyn remained happily married for many more years.

Chapter 8

The Transformation

*I know that there is nothing better for people than
to be happy and to do good while they live.*

ECCLESIASTES 3:12

Approximately ten years ago

> **DISPATCHER:** "Request for first aid at the Pine Cove Apartments,
> Building 3, Apartment B for an unresponsive male."

I groaned as I rolled out of bed. So much for sleeping in this weekend.
I swished some mouthwash before rushing out the door. On the way
to the first aid building, my pager activated again.

> **DISPATCHER:** "Update. As per patrols on scene, expedite. Patient
> is unresponsive, breathing, weak pulse."

I rushed into the squad building and joined Mason Chapman and
Archie Harris. "It sounds serious. I'll drive," Archie said.

Mason climbed in next to him, and I stepped into the back of the
ambulance so I could start gathering our equipment. When Mason

isn't working as an auto mechanic at a local garage, he uses his skills to keep our ambulances in good condition.

Archie called our rig in service, and a few minutes later we pulled up in front of the Pine Cove Apartment Complex. I carried the first aid bag and suction, while Mason grabbed the defibrillator and clipboard. Crisp autumn leaves tumbled along the concrete sidewalk, crunching under my feet as I hustled after Mason.

"The call is on the first floor," he said.

We climbed two steps and entered a breezeway. The door to the second apartment on the right was propped open. We stepped inside, following the sound of voices to the rear bedroom. The smell of stale cigarettes mixed with body odor hung heavy in the air. I stopped breathing through my nose and started breathing through my mouth. A glass half full of a dark-colored liquor sat precariously on the edge of a night table, piled high with old magazines and used tissues.

Officer Brad Sims knelt next to a middle-aged unconscious male who lay on the floor next to a bed. The patient wore a white tank top and faded plaid pajama bottoms. Perspiration shone on his pale face. Tattoos coursed the length of his left arm from shoulder to wrist. A concerned-looking man who appeared to be about 50 hovered close by.

Officer Sims paused his assessment to look up at us. "Our patient is Calvin Jacobs. He's totally out right now. This is his roommate, Trevor. He woke up when he heard a loud bang and came in to see what was going on. He found Calvin unconscious on the floor and dialed 911 right away."

Trevor took a step closer. "At first, I thought maybe he'd been drinking, but I don't think that's it. He drinks, but he doesn't get like this."

Mason began checking Calvin's vital signs. "His blood pressure is low, 92 over 60. His pulse is 98, regular but weak. His pulse ox is 96 percent, and his respiratory rate is 20."

"We can bring him out on the reeves. I'll go get it," Archie said. A reeves is a flexible, portable, lightweight stretcher that can be used to move patients during medical emergencies. It has multiple handholds so numerous rescuers can lift together.

When Archie returned, we lined the reeves with a sheet and rolled Calvin onto it. He remained unresponsive throughout the move. I wasn't sure what could be causing his illness. He didn't have a history of seizures or syncope. He didn't demonstrate signs of an opioid overdose. The emergency department physician would have to perform a thorough investigation to uncover the source of Calvin's decreased level of responsiveness.

The paramedics from the hospital were not available, so we lifted Calvin onto our stretcher and loaded him into our ambulance. His condition remained the same throughout our trip to the hospital. He didn't improve, but at least he didn't worsen either. After we dropped him off, I wouldn't think about him again for the next ten years.

. . . .

I glanced at my physical therapy schedule and smiled. My next patient, Calvin, was a pleasure to work with. When I was with him, I scarcely felt like I was working. I admired his friendliness, openness, and passion for helping others in his community. I knew he volunteered at a local food pantry. He also helped older community members by driving them to doctors' appointments. Truly an all-around nice guy. At age 57, he appeared to have his priorities in order, and they mostly involved caring for others. Since I'd met him, I'd been nagged by the feeling I'd met him before. I just couldn't quite place him.

Calvin ambled into the PT department. I'd been seeing him for the past two weeks for right ankle pain. A month ago, he twisted his ankle when he missed a curb. He wore an air cast for two weeks, and then his doctor referred him for a physical therapy evaluation. Over the past two weeks, the swelling improved and his pain lessened. Overall, he was making good progress. On the first day of PT, he told me his goal was to be able to tolerate standing longer so he could return to volunteering at the food pantry and be able to serve lunch again. Today, he walked in using a straight cane to aid him. He smiled brightly. "Look, no more crutches."

I beamed. "That's terrific. We'll have you back to volunteering in no time."

"That would be great. I puttered around at the food pantry a little yesterday, but I still can't stand on my feet for that long."

After Calvin lay down on our treatment plinth, I applied massage cream to his right ankle. "How long have you been volunteering at the pantry?"

Calvin scratched his head. "Now, lemme see. It's been eight years, eleven months, and six days."

I paused from massaging. "Wow. How do you recall the date so precisely?"

"I began working there exactly one year to the day after my transformation."

He had me at transformation. "May I ask what happened?"

"I wasn't always nice, you know. I guess I was what one might call a bad guy."

I shook my head in disbelief. Calvin was so kind. He made it a point to say hello to the other patients and staff. But he didn't just talk the talk. He walked the walk.

"I can tell you doubt me. I used to be a rough and tough twenty-year-old, and I thought I had the whole world figured out," Calvin said.

. . . .

Years ago

Calvin pulled his cap down over his face as he entered the back alley. He smiled crookedly. Boy, had his mom been wrong in saying he had to finish high school if he ever wanted to accomplish anything in life. If he ever wanted to earn a decent living. Well, he was doing very nicely, thank you. Enough money to get new wheels, pay for his apartment, order takeout to his heart's content. He learned from an early age that crime pays.

He liked to think of himself as a middleman. He bought from the big drug cartels, then sold to guys on the street. He had lots of regular customers. They paid him handsomely for the goods. If they didn't, he "convinced them" it would be best if they did. A black eye or bloody nose was usually enough to motivate them to figure out a way to pay up.

Calvin slipped further into the darkness of the alley. He found the old guy he was looking for, Jimmy, lying on the ground in the back corner of the alley next to a putrid-smelling garbage can. His usual spot. Calvin couldn't understand how he could stand the odor. He figured the guy's sense of smell must have bitten the dust years ago.

Jimmy's eyes were closed. Calvin shook his shoulder to wake him up. He avoided hanging out here longer than necessary. He made sure to always stay a few steps ahead of the cops. He'd known a few guys over the years who got careless. They paid for it, ending up doing time in the slammer.

Jimmy's eyes remained closed. Calvin shook him harder. No response. His skin felt cold to the touch. Calvin swore a string of expletives and felt Jimmy's pulse. *None.* Jimmy was stone-dead. Calvin frowned in disgust. He hated losing customers.

Calvin checked Jimmy's pockets and liberated him of a wad of cash. Jimmy owed him. Not to mention, he was dead now. He wouldn't need money where he was going.

. . . .

Years passed. Calvin's lucrative drug business faltered. He needed cash. Fast. He owed money to some guys who meant business. If he didn't pay them, they'd practice their boxing moves. On his face.

He wasn't sure how to get the money. One thing he did know was he didn't want to end up in the "big house" again. He'd spent a few years locked up and swore last time he was released he'd never go back.

. . . .

Calvin lay in bed, staring at the ceiling. His TV was broken. It had been for a year. He reached toward his night table and grabbed his rum and coke. He took a swig, but even that wasn't enough to ease his discomfort. He hadn't felt well for the past few weeks. He put the glass back, closed his eyes, and fell into a fitful sleep.

Toward daybreak, Calvin awoke when he heard an unusual sound. He opened his eyes, but no one was there.

Was his roommate, Trevor, trying to wake him up? He'd been living with him for the past few years. They got along well, stayed out of each other's business. They both preferred it that way.

Calvin tried to move, but a heavy lead blanket had been tossed over him. At least, that's what it felt like. His arms, legs, head…everything felt so *heavy*. Impossible to move. He felt like he was completely paralyzed. Fear snaked its way into his core. *What's happening to me?*

Calvin wasn't the kind of guy who prayed. He wasn't even sure how to. Although he found it nearly impossible to move his arms and legs, he somehow found the power to slide off the bed onto his knees. He began praying in earnest. "Dear Lord, have mercy on a sinner." He continued praying until he slumped unconscious to the ground.

Trevor, hearing a thumping sound, rushed into Calvin's room, saw his roommate on the floor, and dialed 911.

. . . .

"Wow. It sounds like you were touched by the hand of God. What happened then?" I asked.

"I was in a coma for several weeks. It turns out, I was in severe kidney failure. They were barely working at all. I'd felt sick for several weeks, but I had no idea it could be something so serious."

I stretched Calvin's gastrocnemius and soleus muscles. "Thank goodness your roommate found you and called 911." I studied his face closely. It niggled at my memories. "Hey, did you live in the Pine Cove Apartments about ten years ago?"

"I sure did. On the first floor. Why?"

"I finally figured out why you look familiar. I volunteer with the first aid squad. I took you to the hospital that morning."

Calvin's eyes widened in surprise. "What an amazing coincidence. That day marks a turning point in my life. Before that, I did a lot of things I'm not proud of. But on that day, I truly believe I saw the gates of heaven. It changed my life. When I heard the voice say that it wasn't my time, I knew I had to make some serious changes. I saw those gates, and I knew that's where I want to go when my time here is over. I'm much different now. I try to be nice to everyone and help others. God spoke to me, and I listened. I'm fortunate that I got a second chance. I shudder to think what would have happened if I had died that day."

Calvin's experience transformed his life. He became a true believer and modeled his life after Christ. He serves as an inspiration to many who desire to turn their lives around.

Chapter 9

Hoping for a Miracle

The LORD sustains them on their sickbed
and restores them from their bed of illness.

PSALM 41:3

My shift as an outpatient physical therapist ended at one o'clock, and I stepped out the employee entrance onto the brick patio and clicked my keyless entry to unlock my car. A cool late-February breeze nipped the air, trying its hardest to keep spring at bay. I shivered as I slipped behind the driver's seat. I had several errands to run before picking up my kids from school. I reached into my glove compartment and pulled out my first aid pager. Before I could even slip it onto my waistband, it began beeping.

> **DISPATCHER:** "Request for mutual aid at 1127 Rio Grande Drive in Marina Beach for an elderly fall victim with a hip injury."

I don't have a great sense of direction. I know the streets in my own town very well. However, this was a mutual-aid call, meaning it was in a neighboring town. Most likely, the Marina Beach squad was tied up on another first aid call. I'd never heard of Rio Grande Drive and so plugged the address into my GPS. It looked like it was in a residential neighborhood nestled between Route 65 and Route 13, not too far from the marina. I pass through that area on my way home. I heard Jessie Barnes tell the dispatcher the rig was in service, so I decided to meet the crew at the scene.

After several minutes of highway driving, I veered off and weaved through a bunch of tree-lined side streets before parking across the street from a maroon raised ranch with a quaint wraparound porch. I reached into my cupholder, donned a pair of vinyl gloves (yes, I keep a supply in my cupholder), and headed up the slate walkway. I noted a Marina Beach patrol car parked in front of the house. They'd left enough room for the ambulance to fit behind.

Before I could ring the front doorbell, the door swung open. My eyes widened in surprise.

"Hi, Mr. Beetle."

Although Mr. Beetle was pushing 85, he sported a full head of wavy gray hair. "Why, Andrea, I'm so glad you came. Harriet fell, and I think she may have broken her hip. Follow me, she's in the kitchen."

I couldn't help but be shocked by the amazing coincidence. Harriet Beetle was one of my former physical therapy outpatients. I'd seen her several years ago when her low-back pain acted up. A few months ago, I worked with her on improving her balance and gait. She'd become unsteady on her feet, and I transitioned her from walking with a single-point cane to a rolling walker.

Normally, I wouldn't be responding to an emergency call in this particular town. Now, here I was, and in a town of many thousands, I knew the patient! Harriet possessed a sparkling wit that drew people to her. She's the type of person that, once you meet, you like instantly. I fervently hoped she'd just bruised her hip and not broken it, since fractured hips can spell big problems for elderly folks. However, I knew with a history of osteoporosis, the odds were stacked against her.

What Harriet lacked in size, she made up for in strength and determination. As I rounded the corner from the kitchen into a cozy family room, I spotted her lying on her right side, close to a wooden coffee table with a glass top.

"Mrs. Beetle, I wanted to see you again, but not like this," I blurted out.

"Andrea, I was praying it would be you who came to help me because I know you ride with the ambulance. I'm so mad at myself! Please don't yell at me. I usually use the walker, but I was just going from the kitchen to here, and I forgot. Then I tripped, and down I went like the Titanic. Well, on second thought, I went down a lot faster than the Titanic did. But you get the idea."

I knelt in front of Harriet. "I just got off work, and my pager beeped as soon as I got in my car. You have good timing." I began gently checking her hips and pelvis. The left foot turned outward, indicating a possible fracture.

"I told Honey you would come." (Harriet always calls her husband Honey. I'm not sure what his real first name is.)

"I couldn't believe it when he opened the front door for me. I'm actually on the Pine Cove First Aid Squad. We're just here because Marina Beach must have been busy on another call." I pulled out a blood-pressure cuff from my first aid kit and began checking her vital signs.

"Well, as soon as I fell, I knew right away I needed an ambulance. I'm glad you came to get me off this stupid floor," Harriet said.

I checked her radial pulse, noting it to be strong and regular. "I'm glad I'm here."

Soon, Jessie, along with Colin Branigan, arrived. We used a scoop (stretcher that splits into two pieces lengthwise) to lift Harriet off the floor and onto our stretcher. From there, we rolled her into the ambulance. Soon, we were on the way to the emergency department.

Harriet frowned. "At my age, I hate the thought of undergoing surgery. The anesthesia could really throw me for a loop."

I see Harriet and her husband at church from time to time and know they're deeply spiritual. I squeezed her forearm, and she clasped my hand tightly.

"Please say a prayer for me," she said. "It'll be a miracle if it's not broken."

"I definitely will. You're one of the strongest people I know. Hopefully, you didn't hurt your floor when you fell."

Harriet smiled. "Ha-ha. Well, that floor needs to be replaced anyway."

Soon, we arrived at the emergency department and transferred care over to the triage nurse Maggie Summers and her team. I bid Harriet goodbye and promised to keep in touch.

Harriet waved. "I might need you again in physical therapy when this is all over."

. . . .

The rest of the day passed in a blur: picking up the children from school, caring for the dogs, making dinner, packing lunches for the next day. Soon it was almost ten o'clock. My duty crew starts officially at ten, meaning I'm obligated to respond between the hours of 10:00 p.m. and 6:00 a.m. Tonight, I hoped for a quiet night with *no* rescue calls. Sometimes, especially in the quiet winter months, we get lucky. Everyone stays healthy and safely nestled in their beds. Since I could hear the winter winds howling, I wanted to stay tucked in my warm bed for the night.

Alas, it was not to be. My pager went off at 10:00 p.m. on the nose. Nothing like not having to worry about the suspense of whether you'll have a crew call or not. Now, a mere few seconds into my crew night, I found myself slipping on a pair of sneakers and tugging on my winter coat.

DISPATCHER: "Request for mutual aid in Pebble Lake at 65 Green Street in the garage apartment in the rear of the residence for unresponsive, not breathing."

Two mutual-aid calls in less than 12 hours! This one wasn't in Marina Beach, but rather in Pebble Lake, a town not far from Pine Cove. When I arrived at the first aid building, Jose Sanchez was pulling the ambulance out of the building onto the front apron. Jose retired a few years ago from a long career in politics. He rolled down the window when he saw me approaching. "Hop in."

I didn't have to be asked twice. I was eager to get out of the winter cold before it seeped into my bones. *Permanently.* I slipped into the front passenger seat and yanked the door shut behind me.

Donna Ferlise climbed in the back of the rig. "I was listening on my scanner. The paramedics are on the scene." That meant the medics were already providing advanced life support.

I clicked my seat belt. "That's good. Have we gotten a patient update yet?"

"It's a 26-year-old male. He's still unresponsive," Jose said. Once Donna was safely seated, he called our unit in service and headed toward Pebble Lake.

"Green Street is going to be your second left," I said, zipping up my coat all the way and then donning a pair of gloves. As we rounded the corner, I could tell by the flashing lights that numerous emergency vehicles were already on the scene. Once we parked, Donna and I pulled the stretcher out of the rig and loaded our first aid bag and other medical equipment on top. We rolled it down a long gravel driveway toward the garage. A few times, the wheels got stuck in several deep, half-frozen ruts. We jerked the stretcher out of the grooves and headed toward the outdoor flight of stairs that led to the upstairs apartment.

Despite the cold, the door to the apartment stood wide open. Though we were still outside, a heavy odor wafted over us. It took me a few seconds to identify it. *Dog. Wet dog. Very wet dog.* Not the kind of scent you want to bottle up and sell as a perfume.

We hurried up the steps to see what we could do to help. The higher we climbed, the stronger the smell. Paramedics Kennisha Smythe and Arthur Williamson, along with numerous Pebble Lake patrol officers, crowded around a young man who lay unresponsive on the floor. I could see he had thick brown hair that covered his ears. His face glistened a ghastly pale, his eyes open yet unseeing. He wore a white tank-style undershirt with navy boxer shorts. Tattoos covered the parts of his body I could see.

Kennisha looked up as we entered. "Hi, guys. Thanks for coming out. This is Barry Zales and his girlfriend, Ronda. Barry just moved into Ronda's apartment yesterday. She heard him make an odd gasping noise and ran in to check on him. She found him unresponsive and not breathing, so she dialed 911."

Ronda stepped forward, grabbing a black-and-white mutt by the scruff of his neck as he attempted to dart by. "Barry takes a hit of heroin every day. He must have taken one right before I found him."

I felt something large and furry brush up against the back of my legs. I stepped to the side, noting it was a yellow lab mix. *Two dogs.*

Kennisha squeezed the bag portion of a bag valve mask (BVM), providing rescue breaths at a rate of one every five seconds. "The police gave him one dose of intranasal naloxone before we arrived. The last dose was five minutes ago. His respirations are about four, so we've been assisting his respirations and we're about to give him another dose of Narcan."

I nodded. "Just let us know what you need." A blur of black flew by my peripheral vision. I turned to discover its source. A black shepherd mix. *Three dogs.*

Piles of junk were crammed along the walls. I wasn't sure if they were old piles of stuff or if they were Barry's. Faded wallpaper, a sign of better times long ago, was peeling off the walls in numerous spots. A few baseball-size holes in the drywall didn't help to create a warm, inviting ambiance either. A beige threadbare carpet blushed as it struggled to cover up the plywood flooring beneath.

Ronda picked up a rawhide dog bone from the floor and placed it on a milk crate that was doubling as an end table. "I asked Barry to move in with me so I could keep a better eye on him. I was afraid something like this might happen. I didn't expect it quite this soon."

I heard a yowling noise coming from the kitchen. "Be quiet, Boo," Ronda said. She reached over a wooden-and-mesh gate to pick up a small Chihuahua mix. *Four dogs.*

I turned my attention back to Barry. Arthur gave him another dose of naloxone, and within less than a minute, the patient began moaning, softly at first, then steadily louder.

"He's coming around," Arthur said. "His respirations are improving too. We can switch him over to a non-rebreather."

I pulled a non-rebreather mask out of the top of our green respiratory first aid bag and connected it to an oxygen tank. I turned the flowmeter to 15 liters per minute and placed my finger over the small hole at the base of the mask until the bag fully inflated. As I leaned over and passed it to Kennisha, something knocked against my arm. Something about 45 pounds, with long white hair. *Five dogs. That's a lot of dogs for one small apartment. No wonder it reeks in here.*

Barry progressed from unresponsive to fully alert over the next minute or so. He sat bolt upright, tugging at the oxygen mask. He scowled when he caught sight of us. "I'm fine."

Arthur supported Barry by the shoulders. "You had a period of time in which you weren't breathing. We'd like to take you to the hospital to get checked out."

I half expected Barry to resist, but he merely shrugged. "Okay."

"There's a new program for people struggling with drugs. Would you like more information about it?" Kennisha asked.

Barry shook his head. "No, I'm good."

"No, you're not good," Ronda said. "You're in a class right now and you still take a hit every day." She turned toward us and rolled her eyes. "It'd take a miracle for him to quit."

Barry clenched his jaw. "This only happened because I used a different dealer today. I won't make that mistake again."

Arthur guided Barry down the stairs, and we buckled him into our stretcher. Jose resumed his place behind the wheel as Kennisha, Donna, and I accompanied our reluctant patient to the hospital.

I thought back to the first aid call for Harriet Beetle earlier that day. She'd said it'd take a miracle for her hip to not be broken. Now, Barry's girlfriend said it would take a miracle for him to quit abusing drugs. Two people in vastly different circumstances, yet each hoping for a miracle.

At the time I didn't know it, but hope for a much bigger miracle was only two nights away.

Two nights later

I was startled awake from a deep dreamless sleep when my pager began blaring (I always turn it up to the highest volume at night so I won't sleep through an alarm).

> **DISPATCHER:** "Request for first aid for a twenty-five-year-old male who is unresponsive, possibly not breathing."

Oh no, not again. Not another overdose. "Possibly not breathing" and "unresponsive" in a young person are red flags, as respiratory depression and a decreased level of responsiveness are part of the overdose triad (the third being pinpoint pupils).

Knowing this could be a life-and-death emergency, I hustled to the first aid squad building. When I arrived, Helen McGuire was pulling the ambulance onto the front apron and Colin Branigan was climbing into the front passenger seat. I opened the rear door and scooted in just before Archie Harris. Archie's been volunteering with the rescue squad for many years. Now, his expertise would come in handy. Jose Sanchez climbed in too, and we were on our way.

Helen keyed the mic. "We're in service, responding to Clementine Road."

"Be advised, expedite. The patient is currently not breathing and has no pulse. Patrols are beginning CPR," dispatcher Jerome Franklin replied.

Helen briefly paused the siren. "Received. What's the ETA for the medics?"

"Ten minutes," Franklin said.

I busied myself gathering items such as the defibrillator, suction, and naloxone. I wasn't sure what we'd be facing exactly but wanted to make sure we had every possible means available at our fingertips to help this young man.

Jose had responded to the overdose call two nights ago as well. "I wonder if this fellow overdosed," he said. "Maybe there's a bad batch of heroin in the area." Sometimes heroin is mixed with fentanyl, which makes it more potent and hence more deadly.

I grabbed a small bottle of sterile water to accompany the suction unit. "I was wondering the same thing."

"Such a shame, so many drug-related deaths in the news lately," Archie said.

I began jotting down the information I already knew, such as the time of dispatch, location, and nature of the call.

"It's going to be on your right," Helen said as we pulled up in front of a two-story Colonial.

The five of us hurried across the front lawn, through the open door, and into the foyer. I could hear the voice prompts of the SAED (semi-automatic defibrillator) and followed the sound to a rear first-floor bedroom.

My eyes were drawn to a young man with sandy blond hair who lay flat on his back not far from his bed. A gray-and-white comforter lay on the ground nearby, as if he'd gotten out of bed in a hurry, covers and all. Blank, unseeing brown eyes stood out from the man's chalky white face. Defibrillation pads clung to his bare chest, as if hoping to get an opportunity to resuscitate him. Officer Jack Endicott performed vigorous chest compressions, while Officer Brad Sims used a bag valve mask (BVM) to perform rescue breathing.

A petite woman with shoulder-length wavy brown hair, probably 50 years old or so, stood a few steps off to the side. From her tearful face and shocked expression, I assumed it must be the young man's mother. A small, fluffy white Maltese sat next to her, whining softly.

Officer Endicott spoke while continuing to compress the man's chest. "This is Dan Paxton and his mother. Dan went out to dinner and a movie earlier tonight with his friends. He went to bed around midnight, and at that time, his mother said he seemed fine. He woke her up a few minutes ago, yelling for help."

Mrs. Paxton took a small step forward. "When I rushed in, he was sitting on the edge of his bed clutching his chest. He said, 'Mom, I think I'm having a heart attack.' He said he felt like his heart was beating so hard that his chest might explode. I called 911 right away. When I came back, he'd fallen backwards onto the bed." At that point, her voice wavered. "I couldn't wake him up."

Jose pulled out an oropharyngeal airway and placed it alongside Dan's face, measuring from the tip of his ear to the corner of his mouth. "Any chance he overdosed? Have you given Narcan?" he asked as he deftly inserted the airway.

Mrs. Paxton shook her head vehemently. "No, Dan doesn't drink or do any drugs. He's actually under the care of a cardiologist. He wore a Holter monitor last week, and we're supposed to go back to the doctor next week to find out the results."

I could see saliva bubbling from the corner of Dan's mouth. I began assembling the suction unit, attaching the tubing and Yankauer catheter and running sterile water through the line.

"We analyzed with the defibrillator once, but there was no shock advised. We're due to try again now," Officer Sims said. He pressed the analyze button, and I held my breath. *This is such a young man. Please, God, let this work.* "Press to shock," the SAED prompted. Officer Sims pressed the shock button, and potentially life-saving joules of energy coursed through Dan's chest.

Helen placed two fingers on Dan's carotid artery. "No pulse. Continue CPR." I swallowed my disappointment.

Colin slid next to Dan's chest and took over chest compressions, while Helen began assisting with the BVM. She paused briefly to allow me to suction Dan's mouth. I used a figure-eight technique, suctioning for 15 seconds.

"What were Dan's symptoms that caused him to go to a cardiologist?" I asked.

"He had several dizzy spells in which he felt like his heart was racing," Mrs. Paxton said. "The first time, we drove him to the emergency department. By the time we got there, the spell was over, and the doctor didn't see anything wrong on the EKG. The doctor referred him to a cardiologist, and my husband took him there two weeks ago. While Dan was there, he felt okay. That's why the doctor sent him home with the heart monitor to wear for a week. We just dropped it back off the other day, so they have a chance to analyze it before our next appointment."

"Does he have any other past medical history?" I asked, checking the oxygen gauge to make sure we still had adequate oxygen in the tank.

"Just childhood asthma, but he outgrew that."

I jotted down what Mrs. Paxton said on our notepad. "Does he take any medications? Is he allergic to any that you know of?"

"No. Other than this recent heart problem, he's been healthy. It all sort of came out of the blue. He ran track in high school and never had a problem."

"It's time to analyze again," Officer Sims said. The defibrillator began making a whirring noise as it built up a charge. "Everybody clear. I'm going to shock," he said, waving his arm over the length of Dan's body to make sure no one was inadvertently touching him. Dan's young body jerked from the shock's energy. *Would it work?*

"I've got a strong carotid now. Hold compressions," Helen said. Although Dan's heart now beat again, he still wasn't breathing. Helen and Officer Endicott continued providing rescue breathing with the BVM. Dan's face remained as pale as a fresh winter's snow, and I hoped a glow the shade of cherry blossoms might soon infuse his cheeks.

"I'll get the backboard and stretcher ready," Archie said, slipping out of the room. Now that Dan had a pulse, we'd definitely be transporting him to the hospital. Nowadays, if we can't get a return of pulses in the home, the paramedics will pronounce a person deceased at the scene.

Seconds later, paramedics Kennisha Smythe and Arthur Williamson arrived. Helen quickly updated them regarding Dan's situation.

"See if you can get a set of vital signs for me," Kennisha said.

Helen attached a blood-pressure cuff to Dan's right arm. "His blood pressure is 138 over 100, and his radial pulse is 200 and strong."

Arthur knelt by Dan's head and prepared to intubate him. Intubate means to insert an endotracheal tube into the mouth and down the airway to hold it open.

I noticed that blood began trickling from the corner of Dan's mouth. When I peered closer, I could see he'd begun clenching his jaw. Perhaps he'd bitten his tongue. I reinserted the suction catheter and removed the blood from his oral cavity.

"He's beginning to breath on his own," Arthur said. "Let me call the doc and see how he wants us to proceed. Maybe he'll say to hold off on intubating." He pulled out his cell phone, stepped out of the room, and began discussing the case with his medical director.

"I'm going to gather a few things from upstairs," Mrs. Paxton said. "Is it okay if I ride with you? I'm not up to driving myself."

"Of course. You can sit in the front seat," Jose replied. We often let family members ride in the front passenger seat of the ambulance on the way to the hospital, allowing them to stay as close as possible to their loved ones.

"Thank you," she said. She picked up the Maltese, kissing the top of its head while carrying it out of the room and upstairs. I knew it must be taking a great effort to hold herself together under the strain of her son's sudden collapse.

Although Dan's heart now beat independently, and he was trying to breathe on his own, he remained completely unresponsive.

Kennisha shined a penlight into Dan's eyes. "He doesn't have corneal reflexes. That's a bad sign. He might have brain damage."

Here we are again, just two days later, hoping for another miracle.

Arthur reentered the room. "The doc said to hold off on intubating for now. Let's get him packaged up and get rolling."

Archie slid the backboard alongside Dan. We carefully rolled him to one side using a log-roll technique and placed the board underneath him. We needed the firm surface of the spine board under him in case he lost his pulse again. In that case, we'd need to resume chest compressions.

Once we placed Dan into the ambulance, Helen returned to the driver's seat. Colin offered to drive the paramedic rig so both Arthur and Kennisha could ride with the patient.

"I'll stay back in case we have another call," Jose said.

Archie and I climbed into the back of the ambulance with Dan, and I switched the portable oxygen over to our main onboard tank. Arthur sat in the captain's chair by Dan's head so he could closely monitor his airway. Dan's heart rate remained abnormally high, ranging from 180-200, but much better than no pulse!

Mrs. Paxton sat in the front passenger seat next to Helen, her head craned to the left so she could keep watch over her son. Fortunately, Dan kept breathing on his own and maintained his heart rate on the trip to the hospital. Once we arrived, the triage nurse met us at the door and directed us to a room in the rear of the emergency department. Things happened quickly after that. A team of healthcare professionals—a physician, nurses, technicians, and a respiratory therapist—took over care of Dan. As I left the ED, I said a silent prayer that Dan would make a full recovery.

Two days later

While working as a physical therapist, I learned Harriet Beetle sustained a slight pelvic fracture that didn't require surgery. Much better than a hip fracture! She'd be spending the next few weeks in a rehab facility, and then I'd get to see her in outpatient physical therapy again.

After work, I ran into Helen at the post office. "Any word on how Dan is doing?" I held my breath, wanting to hear good news but fearing it might not be.

"Well, after we left, they intubated him and placed him on hypothermal therapy," she said. "He's still unresponsive, and they're not sure if he has neurological deficits."

Therapeutic hypothermia, or targeted temperature management, is sometimes used after a person suffers cardiac arrest without regaining consciousness. The hope is that it will reduce tissue injury after a period of reduced blood flow to the brain. This treatment reduces the oxygen requirement of the brain and may reduce damage done by free radicals.

It wasn't the good news I'd prayed for. But at least there was hope. Dan was alive, and he still needed a miracle.

Three days later

This time, it wasn't a young man like Dan Paxton or Barry Zales who was in medical distress. Rather, it was an 80-year-old man who smoked too much weed in a restaurant parking lot, went inside, stared off into space for 30 seconds, then fell back, hit his head, and stopped breathing. We put in a nasal airway and performed rescue breathing. By the time we got him into the ambulance, he came around and began speaking. Since we had plenty of other members on the call, I stayed back to pick up my son from baseball practice.

"Hey, did you hear the good news about Dan Paxton?" Officer Brad Sims asked as the ambulance pulled away.

My heart lifted with hope. "No, what?"

Brad smiled. "He's off the vent, fully alert, with no neurological deficits."

God is good. A miracle in action.

Chapter 10

The First to Cast a Stone

*When they kept on questioning him, he straightened
up and said to them, "Let any one of you who is
without sin be the first to throw a stone at her."*

JOHN 8:7

Warm rays of the early autumn sun cast a bright glow as if to deny
that colder fall days lurked just around the corner. As I walked
our Belgian shepherd, Montana, with my family, my pager broke the
tranquility.

> **DISPATCHER:** "Request for mutual aid to 1840 Route 12 at the Bass
> Creek Apartments for an unconscious male, breathing at this
> time, possible overdose."

Bass Creek, a neighbor of Pine Cove, occasionally requests our
squad for mutual-aid assistance when their own rigs are tied up. The
mutual-aid system strengthens the volunteer network, providing depth
of coverage. I've driven by the Bass Creek Apartments a bunch of times,
though I've never been inside one of the apartments.

"Can you take the dog home?" I asked. "I'm going to run back and
get my car so I can answer the call." My kids nodded, used to me rushing off to respond to emergency calls. "Be ready to go to church as soon
as I get back," I added.

I made an about-face and began hurrying back home. Though I ran just a few blocks, my quads stung as I hopped into the front seat of my minivan. I made a mental note to start exercising more. By the time I began driving, Archie Harris told dispatch he was on the ramp with a crew arriving. Since I knew I wouldn't make the building in time, I drove straight to the apartment complex. I followed the narrow driveway around to the rear and parked in a visitor spot. I noticed two Pine Cove patrol cars were parked in front of one of the apartments, and the patio door stood wide open. Usually when we go to other towns to help out on a call, the police from that town assist us. I figured they must all be busy with other emergencies for our patrols to be responding here as well.

I hurried across the tree-lined parking lot and through the patio door into a dimly lit living room. I could hear voices to my left and hurried along a short, carpeted hallway to a bedroom. A middle-aged man with an incredibly blue face lay on his back. Judging from his cyanosis, I could tell his respiratory effort wasn't adequate. He'd need to be assisted with ventilations. That is, we'd need to use a bag valve mask (BVM) connected to an oxygen tank to help him breathe. Officer Vinnie McGovern had already reached the same conclusion, for he was hooking a BVM up to a portable oxygen tank. Officer McGovern, formerly a corrections officer in South Carolina, relocated to the north to be closer to his family. Now, he's an invaluable part of our EMS family.

Officer Kyle Jamieson knelt next to the victim. He glanced up briefly as I entered. "He's got pinpoint pupils." He carefully inserted the tip of the naloxone nasal spray into the man's nostril and pushed in the plunger. Potentially life-saving medication now had a chance to reverse the effects of any possible opioids the man may have taken. At this point, we weren't exactly sure what ailed the man, but we could take an educated guess. He possessed signs of the opioid overdose triad: pinpoint pupils, poor respiratory effort, and decreased responsiveness. Without rapid administration of naloxone and help breathing, this man could die. Thank goodness someone called 911.

Sometimes people think as long as you give an overdose victim naloxone, they'll be okay. This simply isn't true. Naloxone (better known by its trade name Narcan) is best administered while a person still has a heartbeat. If the person stops breathing, soon the heart will stop beating. It's harder to resuscitate a person with naloxone once they're clinically dead. Especially if they've been without a pulse for several minutes or more.

Once Kyle finished administering the naloxone, Vinnie placed the mask portion of the BVM over the man's face, holding it tightly to create a good seal. Kyle began squeezing the bag portion once every five seconds.

I glanced around the bedroom. A plaid comforter was half-pulled up on a queen-size bed, revealing rumpled navy sheets. A half-empty water bottle sat on a maple night table, with an empty beer bottle beside it. Heavy curtains blocked much of the September daylight, casting a gloom over the room.

I spotted a woman who looked to be in her forties standing close to the bed. Dyed blond hair was pulled back in a loose ponytail with a few loose tendrils framing her face. She had black smudges under her brown eyes. I wasn't sure if they were from mascara or lack of sleep. She wore a tight-fitting short black skirt with a short-sleeved red top. Black heels completed the outfit. Maybe they had planned to go out to dinner later this evening, until this emergency derailed the outing.

Kyle shifted back on his heels. "All we've got so far is a first name—Jon." He glanced up at the woman. "Lucy, did he snort or inject the heroin?"

Lucy turned pale. "I don't know. I didn't see him do anything. Just drink a few beers, you know?"

"I can take over bagging if you want to take a look around," I offered. "Just let me get a set of vital signs first."

Kyle nodded, so I knelt next to Jon and felt his radial pulse. "His pulse is 94 and weak." I slipped a pulse oximeter onto his middle finger. "His pulse ox is 83 percent." Normal is 98-100 percent. Jon's was dangerously low. I wrapped a blood-pressure cuff around his left upper arm. "The BP is 116 over 88."

I jotted the numbers on a notepad and then began assisting his breathing with the BVM. His face turned less blue due to receiving the supplemental oxygen, but he still had a very poor respiratory effort. If left on his own, his breathing rate was only six breaths per minute. By assisting him with ventilations, we helped ensure his brain was getting enough oxygen to avoid damage.

Lucy reached for the wall to steady herself. "He was sitting on the sofa, and I noticed he began falling over. I asked him if he was okay, and he said yes. But he didn't look okay. I asked him if he was sure he was all right, and he said yes. Then he got to his feet and sort of staggered into the bedroom. He collapsed on the floor. I called 911 right away."

I continued squeezing the BVM. If Jon didn't begin to respond soon, he'd need another dose of Narcan. "Do you know if Jon has any past medical history?"

Lucy pursed her lips. "I don't know."

"Do you know if he's allergic to any medications?" I asked.

"I'm sorry, I'm not sure," Lucy said.

I didn't think too much of the fact that she didn't know. Perhaps they'd just started dating and she didn't know him that well yet. She stepped out of the bedroom and walked down the hallway toward the kitchen.

Kyle checked the oxygen gauge. "You don't get it, do you?"

"Get what?" I asked.

"You know…" Vinnie said.

I shook my head. I definitely didn't know.

"She's a prostitute," Kyle said. I give him credit for not rolling his eyes.

Ohhhhhhhhh. I blushed. "I'm so naive."

That Lucy could be a prostitute hadn't occurred to me. Not even for an instant. Though in my defense, it was a beautiful sunny afternoon. I guess I assumed that kind of stuff happens at night.

I hid my embarrassment by focusing on Jon, who remained completely unresponsive. His heart continued beating but his breathing effort hadn't improved. Vinnie prepared another dose of Narcan and administered it into Jon's left nostril. Hopefully, he'd come around now.

I heard the ambulance call on location through my pager's open channel. A few seconds later, Archie Harris, Ted O'Malley, and Buddy Stone entered the apartment.

"Can you get me a nasal airway?" I asked, then filled them in on Jon's condition. I noticed thick secretions building in Jon's mouth, with saliva bubbling out the corners. "I'll need the suction unit too."

Vinnie inserted the nasal airway, while I prepared the suction unit. Since Jon remained unconscious, he needed help managing his secretions. Otherwise, he could aspirate and develop pneumonia. A minute later, he lifted his head ever so slightly. Perhaps, he was beginning to wake up a bit. His pulse ox increased to 91 percent, dropped back to the 80s, then settled at 92 percent. Better, but not great. His blood pressure stayed basically stable, now 114/76 and his pulse decreased to 86.

Just then, another one of our volunteers, EMT Clint Edwards, entered the bedroom. "Hey, I just heard on the police radio that we're about to get another call." No sooner had he spoken than our pagers went off.

DISPATCHER: "Request for first aid on the boardwalk for a possible broken leg."

"Archie, Clint, and I can handle this one if the rest of you want to cover the other call," I said. Any minute, we'd have the paramedics from the hospital available to help us here.

"Sounds like a plan," Ted said. He and Buddy left, and I turned my attention back to Jon, who began stirring. The Narcan was doing its job, bumping the heroin out of the opioid receptors in his brain.

"I think the medics are pulling up," Clint said. "I'll get the scoop."

A scoop would allow us to lift Jon off the floor and safely move him to our stretcher. As we adjusted the scoop and clipped the ends together, paramedics Paula Pritchard and Ty Fleming entered. Kyle explained Jon's condition and what treatments we'd rendered thus far.

Paula rapidly assessed Jon. "He's going to need more Narcan." She administered 5 mg intravenously, but his condition remained unchanged. Soon, she administered an additional 5 mg. "His breathing is better, so we can switch him to a non-rebreather," she instructed.

I exchanged the BVM for a non-rebreather mask, and we finished securing him to the scoop. Clint and Archie began carrying him outside, where Clint had set up the stretcher near the patio door.

As I gathered our equipment, I noticed Lucy hovering uncertainly next to me. She clasped her hands tightly together in front of her, and I could see they were trembling. "Is he going to be okay?"

I placed the strap of our heavy first aid jump kit over my shoulder. "Yes, he should be. He's starting to come around. You did a really good job today. By calling 911, you saved his life."

I admired that she called for EMS and stayed with Jon until help arrived. Our state's Good Samaritan Overdose Protection Act allows people to call 911 to report an overdose without fear of being arrested for drug possession themselves. But not everyone is aware of this law. Fearing prosecution, some may simply make a run for it, leaving the overdose victim to succumb to possible death.

She looked me in the eye. "Thank you for that." Then she turned and began gathering her belongings.

I made a mental note to make sure to thank God tonight for all the blessings in my life, then hurried outside and thrust the first aid bag into the outer compartment where it belongs. Archie had already climbed into our driver's seat, and Clint took over driving the medic's rig. I settled into the back of the ambulance with Paula and Ty.

Jon mumbled something unintelligible.

"I'm giving another dose of naloxone," Paula said. Despite all the Narcan, Jon remained lethargic. But at least his breathing was improving. I noticed on the medics' monitor that his heart rate was 84 and blood pressure 110/74. *Definitely trending in the right direction.*

Jon's eyes opened, and he studied the inside of the ambulance as his brain assimilated what was going on.

"Is this the first time you've used heroin?" Ty asked him.

Jon nodded. "Yeah, but I've used everything else. I usually have cocaine, oxycodone, and oxycontin. I've already been to rehab like ten times."

"That's quite a tattoo you have on your arm," Paula noted, smoothing the intravenous line.

"That's in memory of my girlfriend. She died of an overdose," he replied, absentmindedly stroking it. "Hey, who called 911 for me?"

I paused writing down his latest vital signs. "Your friend."

Jon raised one eyebrow. "You mean the whore?"

My eyes narrowed. "She saved your life by calling 911. If she hadn't, you'd be dead. It was brave of her to call and risk being arrested."

My words seemed to penetrate through his post-heroin high. I don't think he realized until that moment how close he'd come to passing from this side of the flower beds to the other. "God bless her," he said softly.

Once we arrived at the emergency department, we rolled Jon through the crowded hallways. While the medics gave a report to the triage nurse, I registered him and then we moved him to a hospital stretcher.

Soon, we were on our way back to Pine Cove. I glanced at the clock. I wouldn't have time to go home before church. I texted Rick that I'd meet him and the kids there. They saved me a seat, and I slid in next to them. During the service, I said a silent prayer for Jon and especially for Lucy. My mind drifted to a passage from the Gospel of John.

> When they kept on questioning him, he straightened up and said to them, "Let any one of you who is without sin be the first to throw a stone at her." Again he stooped down and wrote on the ground.

> At this, those who heard began to go away one at a time, the older ones first, until only Jesus was left, with the woman still standing there. Jesus straightened up and asked her, "Woman, where are they? Has no one condemned you?"

> "No one, sir," she said.

"Then neither do I condemn you," Jesus declared. "Go now and leave your life of sin" (John 8:7-11).

I reflected that sometimes our "guardian angels" are not who we expect them to be. Jon's came in the form of a woman from the world's professed "oldest profession."

Chapter 11

Never Too Old for a Miracle

*"The LORD bless you
and keep you."*

NUMBERS 6:24

om, are you okay?" Sharon Cummings asked. Her mother, Edna, 95 years old, coughed a few times and then grew unusually quiet. Sharon crossed the kitchen so she could better see her mother's face. Right away, she noticed Edna's wide eyes and frightened expression. "Are you choking?"

Wordlessly, Edna placed her hand to her throat. Her panicked expression confirmed Sharon's guess. Sharon knew her son had just arrived home from work and gone upstairs.

"Grayson, come quick! Grandma's choking." Sharon picked up the cordless phone and dialed the Pine Cove emergency number.

"Pine Cove Police Department," Dispatcher Jerome Franklin began. Before he could say another word, Sharon interjected, "We need help. My mother's choking. We live at 104 Crestview Drive."

"Stay on the line while I dispatch the first aid and patrols," Jerome said. After notifying the appropriate units, he asked, "Do you know how to do the Heimlich maneuver?"

"My son just came downstairs. Grayson, do you know how to do the Heimlich?"

"Yes, but I've never actually done it on someone," he said, rushing closer to Edna.

"I'm going to talk you through the steps," Jerome said. "First, I want you to…"

. . . .

> **DISPATCHER:** "Request for first aid at 104 Crestview Drive for a 95-year-old female choking victim."

I'd been busy that day working as a physical therapist in an outpatient clinic. After that, I'd responded to a couple of fire calls. One was a general fire alarm that turned out to be a false alarm. Contractors at the home set it off in error. The next was a small brush fire. A bunch of dry autumn leaves somehow ignited. The fire department extinguished it before it became serious. I'd been home for an hour and just finished eating with my family when my pager went off.

"Bye, gotta go. Eat dessert without me," I said as I grabbed my car keys and rushed out the door.

When I arrived at the building, I slid into the driver's seat and pulled the rig out onto the front apron. I picked up the handheld mic to speak with dispatch. "On the ramp, awaiting a crew."

> **DISPATCHER:** "Update on call at 104 Crestview Drive. Family attempting to perform Heimlich maneuver. Patient possibly going unconscious."

Soon, Jessie Barnes, Jose Sanchez, and Ted O'Malley joined me. I flipped on our emergency lights. "In service," I told Jerome.

Many times, a patient coughs up an object or a bystander or family member successfully performs the Heimlich maneuver before we arrive. Sometimes, we get canceled before we even get on location. If someone is choking, it makes sense to call 911 immediately and get emergency care rolling. It's better to have EMS on the way and cancel them than wait too long and realize you need help after all. Approximately 4,000 people die from choking each year in the United States. In fact, it's the fourth leading cause of unintentional death in our country.

I pulled alongside the curb in front of a stately Victorian. "We're on location on Crestview Drive," I said. I noticed two patrol cars parked in front of the home. As I stepped into the home, I spotted Officer Brad Sims and Officer Vinnie McGovern standing alongside an elderly woman seated in an oak chair in her kitchen.

A young man in his early twenties, who I assumed to be our patient's family member, knelt in front of her. A middle-aged woman with kind eyes stood just to their left. With relief, I noted the victim was no longer choking. Instead, she sucked deep breaths of oxygen into her lungs.

"The dispatcher told me how to do the Heimlich maneuver. I just got it out a minute ago," the young man said, his relief palpable.

"You did a great job," Officer Sims said. Turning to us, he continued, "This is Edna, her daughter Sharon, and her grandson Grayson."

Edna squeezed Grayson's forearm and smiled. "Thank you. Just for the record, I never doubted you."

Grayson hugged her. "Thanks, Grandma, but don't do that again. You scared the life out of us."

Edna smiled. "Oh, it would take more than that to finish me off."

"Mom choked on the cheese of a quesadilla. She's never had a problem with swallowing before, so it really caught me off guard," Sharon said.

"I did the Heimlich, and I looked in her mouth and saw it, so I pulled it out," Grayson explained.

Officer McGovern shook Grayson's hand. "You did an outstanding job."

Jessie checked Edna's vital signs and listened to her lungs. "Everything seems okay, but I think it's a good idea for you to go to the hospital and get checked out. They might want to do a chest X-ray."

Edna and her family agreed, so we moved her onto our stretcher and rolled her to the ambulance. As I drove to Bakersville Hospital, I reflected how fortunate that Grayson happened to have been home in time to save his grandmother's life.

Nine months later

Oh no. Not again. Sharon rushed to Edna's side, where she sat at the kitchen table. Edna's lips turned blue as she struggled to get in air. Sharon whipped her cell phone out of her pocket and dialed 911. "My mother is choking…"

. . . .

The much-welcomed sun peeked out from behind gray stratus clouds after a rain-soaked day. Taking advantage of the break in the weather, my husband and I enjoyed a stroll around Pine Cove Lake. Just as we returned home, my pager went off.

> **DISPATCHER:** "Request for first aid at 504 Crestview Drive for a 95-year-old female choking victim."

"I'll make dinner when I get back," I said to Rick as I jogged back to my car. *504 Crestview. The address doesn't ring a bell.* I flipped on my blue light and headed toward the building. I hit the brakes when an old man in a dented blue sedan slowly backed out of his driveway into the road directly in front of me. I took a deep breath, trying to contain my impatience. I'd lose a minute from the delay. Every second counts with choking victims.

> **DISPATCHER:** "Redispatch with an address correction: first aid call is at 104 Crestview Drive for a 95-year-old female choking victim."

All of a sudden, lights and sirens went off. In my head, that is. I recognized the corrected address. I was still about a block from the building when Jessie Barnes called in service. Since I missed the ambulance, I veered direction so I could meet the squad at the scene.

DISPATCHER: "Update for your call at 104 Crestview Drive: object is out of the airway. Patient is alert and conscious but breathing abnormally at this time."

That's a relief. Either a police officer or a family member must have helped Edna get her airway open again. I turned onto Crestview and parked behind the ambulance just in time to see Jessie, Buddy Stone, and Ted O'Malley enter the front door of the Cummings' home. I grabbed a pair of medical gloves from a cubby in my car door and slipped them on as I hustled toward the house. Ted stood near the front porch, preparing the stretcher.

"How's she doing?" I asked.

"I think she's okay. I'm going to wait out here with the stretcher."

I stepped by him into the house and passed through the front foyer into the kitchen. Officer Brad Sims, Officer Vinnie McGovern, Jessie, and Buddy Stone encircled Edna, who sat on a wooden chair in the middle of the kitchen. I looked at her face closely. It was pale, but not blue. She appeared to be getting at least some air.

"She was blue when we got here. We did the Heimlich maneuver and got out a few pieces of chicken," Officers Sims said.

Edna was chewing on what I guessed to be remnants of chicken. Buddy patted her shoulder. "Spit it out into the paper towel."

I spotted Edna's daughter, Sharon, standing next to the kitchen island. "Do you have a bowl? That might give her a better target to spit into," I suggested.

"Sure." Sharon strode across the kitchen, pulled a white, medium-sized bowl from a cabinet, and handed it to me.

I noticed Edna's face now had a dusky hue, and she had a blank stare.

"Jessie, get the BVM," I said.

Edna began to slump over. *She's passing out.* I crouched behind her and wrapped my arms around her torso. "Someone move the chair." Sharon jerked it out of the way. I laid Edna flat on the floor. The dusky hue of her face morphed into a deep blue, revealing her anoxia. She became completely unresponsive, no longer breathing, pulseless. Her airway obstruction must have gone from partial to complete. She was in cardiac arrest.

No way. Not on my watch. My own heart pounding, I knelt alongside her chest and began delivering chest compressions. I counted aloud, "One, and two, and three, and four," as I pressed down on her chest. I felt a crackle under my hands and hoped I hadn't cracked a rib. I paused from counting long enough to say, "Update the medics that CPR is in progress."

"Done," Officer McGovern said. "They have a five-minute ETA."

When I reached 30 compressions, Jessie held the BVM to Edna's face and attempted to give two rescue breaths. "They didn't go in."

I opened Edna's airway by tilting her head back and peered inside her mouth. Something that looked suspiciously like chicken taunted me from the back part of her throat. I reached in and pulled out one piece of chicken. Then a second. And a third. Although food no longer blocked her airway, Edna wasn't breathing yet. I slid my fingers into the groove alongside her neck. "She has a pulse."

Edna took an agonal (gasping breath). Some of her cyanosis receded, replaced by a pinkish hue. Buddy Stone, who had already prepped the portable suction unit, handed it to me. I slipped the rigid Yankauer catheter into Edna's mouth, sweeping inside with a figure-eight technique for 15 seconds. I sucked out abundant bubbling saliva and made sure there was no more chicken residue. As I withdrew it, Edna took another gasping breath.

Ted passed me a nasal cannula hooked up to a portable oxygen tank. "I have it set at 15 liters per minute."

"Thanks." I slipped the prongs of the cannula into Edna's nares, looped the ends around her ears, and cinched it at her neck. This would provide her with passive oxygenation in addition to the oxygen from the BVM.

When I tried to insert an oral airway, Edna gagged, so I couldn't put it in. A good sign, for it meant she might be regaining consciousness. I pulled a nasal airway from our first aid bag, measuring from the side of Edna's nose to the tip of her ear. I began inserting it into her nostril but met resistance half-way. Since she seemed like she was improving, I pulled it back out. I wrapped a blood-pressure cuff around her left arm and inflated it. "Her blood pressure is 134 over 78."

Ted slipped a pulse oximeter onto her middle finger. "Her pulse ox is 98 percent and heart rate 90."

Edna began breathing more effectively on her own. They were no longer gasping, agonal breaths but rather deeper, normal breaths.

"I think we can switch her from the nasal and BVM to a non-rebreather," Jessie suggested.

I nodded, and we made the switch. Next, we rolled Edna onto a backboard and Officers Sims and McGovern carried her from the house outside to the stretcher. Just then, paramedics Ty Fleming and Paula Pritchard arrived. I filled them in on what had transpired thus far.

Ty nodded. "We'll set up in the rig."

I stepped back inside to get our first aid bag from the kitchen floor, then moved out onto the porch. A tremendous wave of relief washed over me. Edna remained unresponsive and certainly wasn't out of the woods yet, but she was *alive*. Sharon stood on the front porch, composing herself. Wordlessly, I reached toward her. We hugged tightly, conveying with our embrace how grateful we both were that things had taken a turn for the better (after the initial turn for the worse). I led her to the front passenger seat of the ambulance, then stepped into the back with Ty, Paula, and Buddy. Jessie sat in our driver's seat, and Ted took over driving the medics' rig.

Just as I sat down in the small side seat next to Edna, her eyes popped open. "Where am I?"

I squeezed her hand to reassure her. "You're in the ambulance. We're taking you to the hospital to get checked out. Your daughter is in the front seat."

Ty sat across from me and began inserting a needle into Edna's vein to establish an intravenous line. "You may feel a pinch."

Edna scowled. "Hey, that really hurts!"

Ty apologized and explained why the IV line is important. "This way, we can give you some fluids."

Edna rolled her eyes. "I have no idea what you're talking about."

I smiled and recalled Edna's keen wit and sense of humor the last time we took her to the hospital. Although she'd stopped breathing and been without oxygen, her brain remained sharp. A very good sign! I slipped my hand into hers, and she gripped it tightly all the way to the hospital.

Once we parked, I helped Sharon out of the front seat and led her around to the back of the ambulance. Ty stood off to the side. "Thank you," she said to him.

"Don't thank me," Ty said. "I didn't do anything. These volunteers just saved your mother's life."

Sharon's eyes welled with tears. "I know." She turned to me, and we exchanged another hug—a big, old-fashioned "thank you God for the miracle we all witnessed today" hug. "My mother is an extremely religious woman."

"Well, I sure am thanking God for helping us today," I replied.

Triage nurse Maggie Summers met us at the emergency room entrance. "Dr. Morgan is waiting for you in room 13."

We rolled Edna down a long corridor to room 13. As a team, we lifted her from our stretcher to the hospital's. Paula gave a report to Dr. Morgan.

"Are you having any trouble breathing?" he asked Edna.

She shook her head. "No."

"Does anything hurt? Do your ribs hurt?" he asked.

"No, I'm okay."

Over my many years of volunteering, I don't recall ever resuscitating someone of the tender age of 95. *Never too old for a miracle.*

A short time later, our squad received a thank-you letter from Sharon and Edna. Their kind words remain one of the greatest gifts I've received in my years of volunteer service.

> Dear First Aid Squad,
>
> We just wanted to thank you so much for saving my mother's life—we will be endeared to you for life. I was amazed how one piece of chicken kebob can change a life. Then with her turning blue and her heart stopping, it was so scary to watch as you stepped in, especially you, Andrea. After 4 weeks in the hospital and rehab, she is back safe and sound with us and doing very well. I was glad she will be with us to celebrate her 96th birthday in a few weeks. I pray for all of you every Sunday at Church. Again, thank you so much for bringing her back to me! Take care and stay well as we are lucky to have all of you in our town. We have enclosed a token of our appreciation.
>
> Thanks again,
> Sharon and Edna Cummings

Six months later

Each year, our volunteer first aid squad holds an annual dinner to celebrate another year of service to our community. This year, our squad invited two special guests to share the evening with us. When Helen told me they RSVP'd yes, I could barely contain my delight.

At last, the big night came. As I watched Edna and Sharon Cummings stroll into the banquet room, my heart filled with joy. Yes, I used the word *stroll*. Edna had turned 96 since the last time I saw her, and yet she didn't even need a cane to help her walk. Once again, I humbly thanked God for allowing me to be a part of something much bigger than me—to be one cog in the wheel of spokes that led to a miraculous rescue.

A year and a half later

One late summer evening, I bumped into Sharon at a candlelight prayer vigil being held on the Pine Cove boardwalk for a friend of mine.

Sharon smiled. "Mom's doing great! She's 97 now."
The miracle of life continues…

Chapter 12

Happy Birthday

The LORD has done it this very day;
let us rejoice today and be glad.

PSALM 118:24

Chauntel Baptiste lay in bed, quietly trying to catch her breath. She wasn't terribly short of breath, but she wasn't at her usual baseline (mildly short of breath) either. This seemed different. She felt dog tired, yet she couldn't fall asleep. Finally, after a half hour, she climbed out of bed and opened the east-facing bedroom window. She hoped the sea breeze would make her drowsy and ease her breathing effort. While standing, she took a puff of her rescue inhaler. She'd suffered from chronic obstructive pulmonary disease (COPD) for more years than she cared to remember.

Today, Chauntel was 89 years, 364 days old. Tomorrow, she looked forward to turning 90. Her son Francois would be visiting. She slipped back under her covers, determined not to let her breathing problem ruin her birthday.

. . . .

The next day

> **DISPATCHER:** "Request for first aid at 1805 Ocean Boulevard for a 90-year-old female with difficulty breathing."

I glanced at my wristwatch, noting it was just past seven o'clock. I'd eaten an early dinner and taken a quick shower. Now, I hurried to the first aid building where I met up with fellow squad members Kit Carmichael and Ted O'Malley. Kit, a financial advisor, joined the squad last year. She slid out of the driver's seat when I arrived. "Would you mind driving?" she asked.

"No, that's fine," I said, slipping behind the wheel. Ted sat next to me. I picked up the mic and flipped on our emergency lights. "We're in service, responding to Ocean Boulevard."

"Received. Your medic unit is responding from Marina Beach with a five-minute ETA," Dispatcher Franklin responded. "The easiest entry will be the rear door of the house."

A couple of minutes later, we pulled up in front of a beautiful gray Victorian with white trim. A stately two-foot-tall stone wall surrounded the property. After I called on location, I let Ted and Kit out so they could start the assessment. Then, I backed the ambulance down a long brick driveway, taking care not to run over the ornamental red-and-white begonias that lined both sides.

Someone had propped open the back door. I stepped inside, listening for voices. I didn't hear any, so I walked through a modern white kitchen and stood at the base of a sweeping wooden staircase with a plush floral runner. Now, the sound of voices drifted down to me. Paramedics Ty Fleming and Paula Pritchard entered the house after me and followed me upstairs.

"I haven't been up yet myself, so I can't tell you much," I said.

I found Kit and Ted with Officer Jack Endicott on the third floor, assessing a frail, elderly woman who sat perched on the edge of her queen-sized bed. Her face was flushed, as though she had a fever. Or maybe the redness was due to the work of breathing.

Kit pumped up a blood-pressure cuff around the woman's upper arm, then released the pressure. "This is Chauntel Baptiste. She has a history of COPD, and she's complaining of mild shortness of breath since last night. Her blood pressure is 190 over 80."

Chauntel glanced up as the medics and I stepped further into the room. "Hello. My goodness, how many of you are there?"

"Enough to make sure you get exceptional care," Ted said, slipping a pulse oximeter onto her middle finger. "The heart rate is 98 and pulse ox is 97 percent."

"When did you start having trouble breathing?" Kit asked.

"I started feeling unwell last night, but I kept hoping it would simply go away. No such luck, however."

A middle-aged man wearing a short-sleeved blue oxford and khakis stepped forward. "I'm Francois, Chauntel's son. Mom didn't want me to call for EMS, but I insisted. She's been a bit short of breath, and I thought it best she gets checked out. She's been putting it off all day, but I finally overruled her and dialed 911."

Ty and Paula took over the patient assessment, so I returned downstairs to set up the stretcher at the back door. I also needed to get the stair chair, a collapsible chair with treads that makes it easier to transport a patient down a flight of stairs. I carried the stair chair upstairs and set it up close to the patient, making sure to give the medics adequate space to perform their assessment. I realized they'd want to give her a breathing treatment before we moved her.

Francois tapped my shoulder. "Do you have a minute to come with me?"

I nodded. "Of course." I expected he was going to lead me to his mother's medications or confide something about her medical condition that he didn't want her to overhear.

I followed him from the bedroom out onto a large open balcony that faced the Atlantic Ocean. He took a deep breath, then slowly released it. "How can you not take a moment to enjoy this view?"

The moon, a giant tangerine, floated above the ocean. Its beams reflected magically across the silent sea, creating a brilliant lit pathway. Almost unreal. Like a giant movie set. Breathtaking.

"Wow, thank you," I murmured. The words seemed an inadequate response for such awe-striking beauty. We stood silent for a moment, soaking in the gift of God's perfection.

I glanced back into the bedroom. Ty and Ted pivoted Chauntel onto the stair chair. Time to say goodbye moon and return to work.

Officer Endicott and Ted maneuvered Chauntel down two flights of stairs. I followed behind, carrying the first aid bag and oxygen tank. Francois trailed behind me.

"I'm the driver," I said. "You can ride in the front seat if you like."

"That would be great. I'm not from around here. When Mom's done, I can call someone to pick us up."

We loaded Chauntel into the back of the ambulance. Ty, Kit, and Ted stayed with her, and Paula took over driving the medic rig. I led Francois to the front passenger seat, then slid into the driver's seat.

"We're transporting one to Bakersville Hospital," I notified dispatch.

The trip to the hospital was uneventful. Soon, we were rolling Chauntel down a long hallway to the registration desk and triage area. Stretchers full of patients filled the area: an older woman wearing a cervical collar, a middle-aged man sleeping off too much booze, a twenty-something with a pillow splint on the left ankle, an older gentleman holding an emesis (vomit) basin, and many more. Concerned family members stood next to them or sat in nearby plastic chairs. Numerous nurses and aides bustled about, attending to the patients' needs.

Ted procured a stretcher from further down the hallway, and we lifted Chauntel from ours onto that one. Kit and I adjusted her blankets and pillows while Ty gave a patient report to triage nurse Maggie Summers.

As Ty wrapped up the patient report, Francois loudly interjected, "It's my mother's birthday."

Maggie, normally no-nonsense and focused, turned toward Chauntel. Without missing a beat, she burst into song. "Happy birthday to you…"

Francois smiled brightly and joined in with a deep, booming, Broadway-quality voice. "Happy birthday to you…"

Several nurses and a bunch of techs gathered around us and we all joined in. Before I knew it, the patients lining the hallways and their families began singing too. A sense of wonder suffused me, and a chill

tickled my spine. Not the bad kind of chill. The kind that acknowl-
edges you are witnessing something truly extraordinary.

Kit turned to me and whispered, "It's like a scene out of a movie."

I couldn't help but agree. I felt like we were part of one of those
flash-mob videos that I've seen on the Internet. But this was not a
rehearsal. It was real. A gift from God that sucked away some of the
pain and glumness from the emergency department and replaced it
with gratitude and joy.

Chauntel beamed, her misery temporarily forgotten. "Well, my
goodness. Thank you, everyone."

"Francois, you have an amazing voice," I said. He smiled and winked
in response. He'd turned an upsetting life event into something more
positive, not just for his mother, but for the other patients and staff as
well.

By volunteering my time that evening to help someone in need,
I became doubly blessed. First, the vision of the striking tangerine
moon. Then, witnessing a birthday miracle. Two gifts that remind me
how blessed I am to have the opportunity to serve my community as
an EMT.

Chapter 13

Piecing It Together

I will instruct you and teach you in the way you should go;
I will counsel you with my loving eye on you.

PSALM 32:8

lexa Tuckerton opened her eyes and blinked. A distinct wave of uneasiness washed over her. *Where am I? This doesn't feel like my bed. And this certainly doesn't look like my bedroom.* Her gaze swept across the dimly lit room. Heavy beige drapes covered what appeared to be sliding patio doors. A sliver of sunlight filtered through the gap between where the ends met in the middle. *What time is it?*

Alexa felt the beginnings of a dull headache, her temples throbbing from confusion and uncertainty. Rolling to her side, she swung her legs over the edge of the bed and sat up, the way her physical therapist taught her to. She leaned over and switched on the lamp on the nightstand next to her bed. Now with the room fully lit, she could study it in more detail. An unfamiliar print of kittens playing with a ball of yarn adorned the wall at the head of the bed. It wasn't hers. She didn't particularly care for felines. She considered herself to be more of a dog person.

She flexed her neck, peeking at her clothing. *Why, I'm not wearing pajamas!* Instead, she wore a knee-length green floral dress with a lacy collar. With a sigh of relief, she realized that the dress, at least, was hers. *But why am I wearing it?* Alexa rose to her feet, drawn toward the glass doors. She pulled the drapes open and stared out at the unfamiliar scene in front of her, trying somewhat unsuccessfully to curb her rising discomfort. The attractive homes across the street didn't evoke even the slightest hint of familiarity.

Once in a while, Alexa forgot things. At the tender age of 87, she figured it was normal. And anyway, several years ago she had to undergo brain surgery (she couldn't recall exactly what it was for). Sometimes she blanked out on a person's name. Or she went into a room to get something but forgot what she wanted when she got there. But nothing like this had ever happened to her before. She'd never woken up in a strange place, uncertain of where she was. She sat in a beige armchair near the window, placing her head between her hands. *Think, think.* Elusive memories filtered in. A dinner party…that's it! She went to a dinner party last night at the Harrington Hotel. She and 17 of her closest friends made it an annual event. Why, they'd been doing it for decades. But how'd she end up in this room?

Alexa knew one thing with certainty. She wanted to go home, right now. She could call a cab. Except…she couldn't remember where she lived. She'd moved several times over the past few years, and now she drew a complete blank.

Of course, my pocketbook! She spotted her bag on a dresser, across from the foot of the bed. Eagerly, she dug into the contents. The purse wasn't very big. Disappointment enveloped her, sucking her toward a void of despondency. Her wallet wasn't in her purse. Nothing to indicate where she lived. *What should I do?*

Alexa didn't have a smartphone. She had an old-fashioned cell phone, the kind you use for emergencies. It didn't have contacts in it or anything like that. *Maybe I can use it to call the police. Maybe they can help me. But what can I say? How mortifying to admit I'm not sure where I live. They'll think I'm nuts.*

An idea slowly formed in her mind. She might be able to get help without admitting she forgot where she belongs.

DISPATCHER: "Request for first aid at the Harrington Hotel in Room 316 for an elderly woman with knee pain."

I glanced at the clock as I wolfed down the last bite of a slice of toast. *7:45 a.m..* I tossed my Belgian shepherd, Montana, a treat. "I promise I'll walk you as soon as I get home."

I hustled to the first aid building. Jessie Barnes sat in the driver's seat and Ted O'Malley in the passenger's seat. I climbed into the back, firmly pulling the door shut behind me.

"We're in service," Jessie told dispatch as he pulled out into the road and headed toward the Harrington Hotel.

"I can't imagine many people are staying there right now. It's off season," Ted said. Pine Cove's hotels tend to be more active in the summer. This cold, crisp winter morning spoke of many more days of chilly weather ahead. Although bright sunlight sparkled on the rippling ocean waves, the water temperature couldn't be more than 50 degrees. Much too cold for a dip. Not to mention the air temp was struggling to get out of the twenties.

Jessie parked in front of the entrance to the Harrington and picked up the hand-held mic. "We're on location."

"I'll hang back with the rig. Just radio if you need anything, and I'll bring it up," Ted said.

I pulled out the frac pack (set of splints for arms and legs) and placed it along with the first aid jump bag on top of the stretcher. Jessie and I rolled it inside and took the elevator to the third floor. As we rolled down the hall toward room 316, I couldn't help but admire the seaside motif. Paintings of sunset beaches, children splashing and frolicking in the waves, and seemingly endless boardwalks. A promise of summers to come.

Officer Ethan Bonilla met us at the entrance to the room. Officer Bonilla worked through the ranks as a Class I and Class II special officer before becoming a patrolman. He spoke in hushed tones. "We have a bit of a problem. Alexa Tuckerton isn't sure where she lives."

I gazed through the doorway and studied the frail elderly woman seated on the edge of a queen-sized bed. The physical therapist in me noted that she sat with good posture, her shoulders back rather than curled forward. Her feet were tucked neatly beneath her, even the right one. If she'd fallen and injured her right knee, she must have somehow been able to return to her bed.

"Did you say Alexa Tuckerton? I took her husband to the hospital many years ago. They live in a pretty white Colonial in the 200 block of Bartholomew Road." I had taken Mr. Tuckerton to the hospital after he fell on the sidewalk across the street from his house. At the time, Alexa wasn't home, so I'd never met her in person.

Jessie shook his head. "She used to live there but moved into a condo complex about a year ago, after her husband passed away."

We stepped across the threshold into the room. Jessie knelt next to Alexa, placing himself at eye level. "I'm Jessie and this is Andrea. We're volunteers on the Pine Cove First Aid Squad. We heard you have right knee pain."

A funny look flashed briefly across Alexa's face. "Yes, it felt stiff when I woke up, but it feels better now. I don't think I need to go to the hospital or anything."

"Well, let's check you out and make sure," Jessie said. He began inspecting Alexa's right knee and checking her vital signs. "No obvious deformity of the knee. Her pulse is 70 and blood pressure is 120 over 80." He winked. "Better than mine. Do you still live at the Pine Cove Condo Complex?"

Alexa flushed. "No, I don't think so. I'm pretty sure I moved somewhere else. Officer Bonilla probably told you already, but I can't remember where I live."

Officer Bonilla took a few steps closer to Alexa. "I tried contacting the front desk, but they aren't sure where Alexa lives. They do know she attended a dinner party here last night."

Alexa nodded. "Yes, 18 of us get together every year to celebrate. We've been doing it for as long as I can remember."

I smiled. "That sounds like a fun tradition. One of our squad members,

Ted O'Malley, is down with the ambulance. He lives in the Pine Cove Condos. Perhaps he knows where you moved after you left there."

Officer Bonilla pulled his portable radio out of its holster. He called the ambulance several times but couldn't get through to Ted. "I'll walk down and ask him."

"Great. While you do that, I'll see how Mrs. Tuckerton does with walking." I'd spotted a rollator walker (the kind with brakes and a seat) off to the side. I rolled it closer. "Let's take a little spin around the room and make sure that right knee is all right."

"Okay, but I'm sure it's fine. A lot of times, I don't even use the walker." She stood up without any assistance, and we began walking toward the far side of the hotel room. Jessie stayed where he was, jotting the information we'd gathered so far onto our run sheet.

Alexa's gait seemed normal. She didn't limp or favor her right leg. "You're walking seems pretty good. Do you have any knee pain now?" I asked.

Alexa paused, letting go of her walker with her right hand. She placed it on my forearm, gently tugging me closer. "I have a confession to make. My right knee feels perfectly fine. It never actually hurt. I made that part up. I only said it because I was too embarrassed to call the police department and admit I don't remember my address. I remember what it looks like where I live, but I just can't recall the name. I'm pretty sure it's an assisted-living place."

I patted her shoulder. "Don't feel bad. I'm sure we'll figure it out. You've lived in Pine Cove for a long time, so I'm sure someone knows where you moved to."

We walked back toward the window, and Alexa sat in an armchair. Just then, Officer Bonilla reentered the room. "Ted recalls you moved to an assisted-living facility not far from here, but he's not sure which one."

"How did you get to the party last night?" I asked. "Did you drive? Get a ride? Take an Uber?"

Alexa scrunched her forehead. "Hank and Laura drove me here. They come to the party every year too. I don't know why they didn't take me home."

Hank and Laura. Hank and Laura. I know an older couple named Hank and Laura. "Is Hank and Laura's last name Wheatley?"

Alexa's eyes widened with surprise. "Why, yes. Do you know them?"

"I sure do. Laura taught my children years ago, and I met Hank through church. I think I have Hank's cell phone number. Let me see…" I pulled out my phone and began spooling through the contacts. *Bingo.* "Let me give them a call."

Alexa sighed with relief. "Thank you. Can you please ask them if they can bring me home now?"

"Sure." I took a few steps back so I could explain the situation to Hank in privacy. I hadn't spoken to him in several years, so my call would probably catch him by surprise. He answered on the second ring. I quickly gave him a rundown on his friend's predicament.

"Yes, Laura and I brought Alexa to the Harrington yesterday, but we were never supposed to be her ride home. I'm sorry we can't take her home now, but we left the party last night a little early so we could hit the road at the crack of dawn. We're out of the state."

I gave Alexa a thumbs-up as I wrapped up my conversation with Hank. "No worries. We can take her home. I'm just glad you could tell us her address."

Officer Bonilla called Alexa's assisted-living facility and asked if someone could meet us in the lobby. We loaded her into our ambulance and delivered her home safe and sound a few short minutes later.

"I can't thank you all enough," Alexa said. "As soon as I get to my apartment, I'll put an index card in my purse with my name and address so this never happens again."

I reflected that even when we find ourselves in a difficult predicament, God sends the resources to help us. This morning was truly a team effort. We were able to pool our information and resources to piece together where Alexa lived and take her home.

· · · · · · · · · · · · ·

Ronald Bossworth groaned as pain ricocheted along the tender tissue near his Foley catheter. The pain had started very late last night but then gradually eased, affording some much-needed sleep after a late night out. Once he woke up, the pain returned with a vengeance. He worried he might be getting another urinary tract infection. At the tender age of 88, he didn't need any more medical issues to add to his growing list.

Since it was a Sunday, Ronald couldn't call his primary care doctor. He lived alone and didn't have family in the area who could take him to an urgent care center. He broke out in a cold sweat, the pain rendering him incapable of walking. He wondered if a person could pass out from pain. Fortunately, his cell phone was in his pocket. He pulled it out and dialed 911. "I need an ambulance…"

. . . .

After the call for Alexa earlier that morning, I grabbed a bite to eat for breakfast and walked my dog. Just as I got back home, my pager went off.

> **DISPATCHER:** "Request for first aid at 204 Bartholomew Road for a medical emergency."

The address rang a bell. I'd been there several years ago for an older gentleman with complications after surgery on his large intestines. He lived on the same street where Alexa Tuckerton, the woman we'd just taken home to her assisted-living facility, used to live. In fact, my friends Hank and Laura Wheatley, the couple that helped us piece together the information from the last call, used to live on that road too.

I arrived at the first aid building at the same time as volunteer squad members Carl Blakely and Kayla Taylor. Carl, a businessman, joined the squad a few years ago when he had a little more time on his hands after he switched jobs and no longer had a long commute to the city. Kayla is a retired dancer. Her family has lived in Pine Cove for many generations. She, like her relatives, enjoys serving the community they love.

"I'll drive," Carl offered, sliding behind the steering wheel. I climbed into the passenger seat next to him, the cold wind blowing the door closed behind me.

"If it's who I think it is, I've had this person before," I said.

"I'm ready back here. You can go," Kayla said after buckling up in the back of the ambulance. "I wonder what the medical emergency is."

Carl called our rig into service, and soon we parked in the driveway of an elegant gray Victorian with white trim. Thin patches of old snow from last week's storm covered the front lawn, but fortunately the front walk remained clear. We pulled out the stretcher and piled our equipment on top. We left the stretcher near the front door, and I made sure to put on the brakes to keep it from rolling away down the gently inclined property.

Officer Vinnie McGovern met us at the entrance, holding the heavy oak door open. An older man with a thick head of snowy white hair sat in a high-backed armchair close to the front door. I recognized him as the man I recalled from a previous call.

"This is Ronald Bossworth," Vinnie said. "He's having a lot of pain from his urinary catheter and would like a ride to the hospital to get checked out."

Carl knelt next to Ronald. "No problem. We can help with that. Can you tell us a little more about what seems to be the trouble this morning?"

"Well, I was fine yesterday evening when I went out to a dinner party. However, by the time I got home, I knew something was wrong. The pain started building in the area around my catheter until it became excruciating. I went to bed and somehow managed to fall asleep, but when I woke up, the pain began kicking again."

Ronald Bossworth was at a dinner party last night?! I wonder... I passed a blood-pressure cuff to Carl. "Did your dinner party happen to be at the Harrington Hotel?"

Ronald's eyes opened wide. "Yes, how did you know?"

"A lucky guess. Were your former neighbors Hank and Laura Wheatley there?" I asked.

Ronald held his arm out so Carl could tighten the cuff. "Yes, they sure were. How do you know them?"

"Old friends," I replied, not wanting to go into detail, instead focusing on his current situation. But I couldn't help but wonder, *What are the odds?* It must have been some party! Eighteen people were there, and we'd already had first aid calls for two of them. Would there be more?

Ronald's condition seemed stable. Kayla jotted down his name, date of birth, and medical history, while Carl and I helped him onto our stretcher. We loaded him into the ambulance and headed toward the emergency department. Although Ronald continued to be in pain, his vital signs were all within normal ranges. At the hospital, they'd determine if his catheter needed to be repositioned or replaced. Or perhaps he had an infection brewing that needed treatment with antibiotics. At least now, Ronald was in the right place to get help with his medical problem.

We made a quick turnaround at the hospital. After we gave the patient report to the triage nurse and wiped down our stretcher and equipment, we headed back toward Pine Cove.

"I'm not sure, but I'm starting to think we may be part of a bad movie plot," I said.

Carl raised his eyebrows. "Why? What do you mean?"

Kayla giggled. "I like bad movies. Tell us more."

I smiled, my active imagination beginning to run wild with possibilities. I explained how our last two patients were both at the same party last night. Coincidence? Or something more?

About halfway back to town, our pagers went off again.

> **DISPATCHER:** "Request for first aid for a 90-year-old female who needs a lift assist. Exact location of call is being determined."

Carl picked up the handheld mic. "We're in service, responding to the lift assist."

I slipped on a pair of vinyl gloves. "What if she went to the party last night too?"

"That would be three in a row. And we could get up to fifteen more!" Kayla exclaimed.

No.

Way.

Not a third one!

"Pine Cove First Aid, you can take a cancel on the lift assist. Patrols will cover," Dispatcher Franklin said.

Now we'd never know if she would have been our third party goer!

Chapter 14

Four-Legged Guardian Angel

*The LORD makes firm the steps
of the one who delights in him;
though he may stumble, he will not fall,
for the LORD upholds him with his hand.*

PSALM 37:23-24

Nine months earlier

No way." Mickey Davis shook his head vehemently. "You know we already have two dogs. We can't handle another one. Anyway, Gina would have a fit." His wife wasn't exactly what you'd call a dog person. She'd grudgingly agreed to two dogs. He worried three might push her over the edge.

"But Mickey, just look at her," his best friend, Jimmy Hudson, implored. "Sure, she's past her prime. But she's a purebred German short-haired pointer."

As if knowing she was auditioning for a part that could determine her future, Blaze stood up and began wagging her tail. She trotted over to where Mickey was sitting and placed her head on his knee.

Mickey tried to steel himself against Blaze's friendly overtures. He really did. Nonetheless, he found himself patting her head. Her fur was sleek and soft, perfect for petting. He knew in a few short weeks, Jimmy would move halfway across the country. The tech company he worked for had been taken over, and his IT position transferred to the new headquarters. He needed a paycheck, so he didn't have much choice. He had to go.

Jimmy ran a hand through his hair. "Listen, it wouldn't be forever. And you'd be doing me a huge favor. I'm starting off in an apartment that doesn't allow pets. But once I get settled into the new routine, I could find a place that would let me keep Blaze. It's a short-term lease, so I can start looking for something pet-friendly right away."

As if on cue, Mickey's beagle, Gus, and shepherd mix, Pinto, rushed onto the deck to receive their fair share of attention. He tossed them each several dog biscuits.

"It'd be an awful lot of dogs for one house, if you know what I mean," Mickey said.

"At least you have a fenced yard. Plenty of room for them to run around. And they all get along so well. I don't want to take her to a shelter. She's eight years old. No one would want her. They'll end up putting her down."

The three dogs did get along quite well. And Mickey knew Jimmy had a good point. Even though she didn't act like one, Blaze could already be considered a "senior dog." Most people wouldn't even consider adopting a big, old canine. Mickey felt himself caving in.

"Promise it's only for three months?"

. . . .

Six months later

Mickey woke up during the night with a serious case of the munchies. He rolled over and glanced at his wife, Gina. She'd been on his case to lose a few pounds. Now that he was 52, he noticed the weight seemed to be going to his midsection a lot faster than it used to (and staying there). He'd been good at eating healthy this week. Lots of salads, low-fat yogurt, salmon, and nuts. So, a little snack now wouldn't hurt, right? He'd earned it. He could practically taste the butter on a bowl of salted, movie-theater microwave popcorn.

He slipped on his robe and slippers. Blaze, who slept on a dog bed next to Mickey's, stood up and followed her temporary owner as he slipped out of the bedroom and headed downstairs.

Jimmy claimed he was still searching for dog-friendly digs but hadn't had any luck yet. Mickey didn't mind. Blaze had grown on him, and he'd gotten used to having her around. Gina still wasn't thrilled (she's more of a cat person), but at least she'd stopped asking when Jimmy was coming to get his dog.

As Mickey passed through the living room, Gus hopped off his cozy spot on the sofa and waddled into the kitchen, his nails clicking his arrival on the tile floor. Pinto, who preferred to curl up on a thick throw rug in front of the fireplace, also followed them to see what the late-night gathering was all about. Mickey reflected that although he'd raised Gus and Pinto from puppyhood, it was Blaze who rarely left his side. *She's probably afraid I might leave her too, like Jimmy.*

Mickey's solo midnight snack blossomed into a foursome. He flipped the kitchen lights onto a dim setting and placed a bag of popcorn into the microwave. While it popped, he poured himself a glass of cold, crisp ginger ale. He patted each dog on the head and tossed them a few treats. He chuckled at their excitement. "No, it's not breakfast time yet."

After devouring his dog treats, Gus grunted and lay down. Pinto wandered over to inspect under the kitchen table, hoping someone left behind some tasty crumbs. Blaze stood by Mickey's side, his self-appointed shadow. The microwave dinged its completion. As Mickey opened the popcorn bag, the scent wafted tantalizingly through the air. He shoved a handful in his mouth as he headed toward a barstool at the end of the kitchen island.

Suddenly, Mickey couldn't breathe. Couldn't cough. He struggled to get in air, frantically trying to dislodge the popcorn that lodged in his airway. He wished he could yell for help, but he couldn't make a sound. Somehow, he'd always pictured people choking in restaurants, where other people could help. What do you do if you're alone and choking? Who does the Heimlich maneuver on you when you're by yourself?

Maybe I can do it to myself. Desperate for air, Mickey thrust his abdomen across the backrest of the barstool. *If I don't get this out of my airway, I'm going to die.* Once, twice, three times he flung himself onto the chairback. The popcorn remained stubbornly stuck.

What else could he do? He staggered backwards, frantically scanning the dimly lit kitchen for some sort of miraculous solution. He didn't find one.

The kitchen grew darker and darker. Mickey was losing the fight, gradually slipping away, losing strength. *So, this is it. This is how I'm going to die.* As he lost consciousness, he pitched forward. His chest struck the floor first, then his chin and face. His head was violently thrust backwards, making a loud snapping noise that only the three dogs could hear.

. . . .

Mickey felt a warm, moist sensation sweeping across his right cheek. His eyes popped open. He felt numb from his shoulders downward, first like an odd buzzing, and then he couldn't feel much of anything at all. Despite his impaired sensation, he sensed he was lying on something hard. It felt like someone was stabbing knives into his neck. Sharp steak knives, not butter knives.

Gradually, Mickey became more aware of his surroundings. He realized he was lying on the kitchen floor. Groggy, he struggled to recall what happened. How long had he been lying here? Memories sneaked back into his consciousness: eating the popcorn, choking, blacking out. Now, he lay face down on the cold floor, his head cocked back and slightly to the right. All at once, he realized he could breathe. He pulled air into his lungs, grateful for the life-giving oxygen.

A yellowish blob about six inches from his face caught his attention. *Yuck, what is that? Did Gus throw up again?* He strained to see the small bumpy mound more clearly. Popcorn! With a start, he realized that when he hit the floor, the sheer force must have propelled it from his airway.

Mickey felt the wet sensation travel across his cheek again. *Blaze!* She'd stayed by his side through the ordeal, licking him and whimpering to wake him up. "There's a good girl. Now, I just need to get up. My neck is killing me."

Mickey's arms felt funny, as if they belonged to someone else. He realized they must be caught beneath him. When he had blacked out, he'd fallen like a tree, unable to put out his hands to protect himself.

Mickey tried to slide his right arm out from under himself but couldn't. Then, he tried moving the left arm. No luck. Had he been lying here unconscious for so long with his arms trapped underneath that they went numb?

Mickey tried to move his right leg. Nothing. Left leg. Zilch. Zero movement. Horror mushroomed within him. *I'm completely paralyzed.* He could move only his eyes and tongue.

Gina can help me. I just need to yell loud enough to wake her up. Even as Mickey formulated the plan, doubt filled him. His wife was a heavy sleeper. She regularly slept through her alarm clock. In fact, loud cracks of thunder didn't even cause her to stir. One time, she slept through a small earthquake.

"Help," he cried. But the earth-shattering yell he envisioned came out more like a loud whisper. If Gina didn't wake from the sound of his fall, she sure wasn't going to hear his feeble call.

He realized the gravity of his situation. Completely paralyzed, hours to go until morning. And since it was a weekend, Gina might sleep in. To make matters worse, Mickey worried about his diabetes. What if his blood sugar got too high or too low? And what about his heart condition? Last year, he suffered a major heart attack. The surgeon ended up rushing him to the operating room and giving him a cardiac stent.

Just then, Blaze's whine caught Mickey's attention. The dog he initially hadn't wanted now stood vigil at his side.

"Hey, buddy, I'm not so good right now."

Blaze's whines grew louder. She punctuated them with several loud barks, as if calling for help.

"That's a girl," Mickey murmured.

He wondered where Gus and Pinto were. He didn't hear any

grunting (Gus) or panting (Pinto). They'd probably gone back to sleep in the living room. Now, his hope for survival hung on a friend's German short-haired pointer.

Blaze continued to whine, interjecting occasional barks. Long minutes passed, stretching into a half hour or more. The dog lay close to Mickey, occasionally licking his cheek. The feeling of the dog's breath on his face brought Mickey comfort. *At least I'm not completely alone.*

Suddenly, the warm breath vanished. Mickey heard the tread of Blaze's feet as she padded away toward the base of the staircase. When she reached it, she unleashed a torrent of thunderous barking. After a few minutes, she returned and licked his face, whining gently as if to say, "I haven't forgotten about you." Then she rushed back to the stairs and began barking again.

This cycle went on for about 15 minutes: barking at the base of the stairs, then returning to check on Mickey. Eventually, Mickey heard Gina call out, "For heaven's sake, would you be quiet?"

At the sound of Gina's voice, Blaze amped up her barking to a frenzy, trying to convince her to come downstairs.

· · · · · · · · · · · · ·

For crying out loud, what in the world is the matter with that dog? Sure, we'll only have her for three months my foot. Now three months have turned into six. And I bet six will turn into nine, then a year. Maybe more.

Gina put a pillow over her head, determined to block out the sound of Blaze's barking. Except, it didn't work. Her barking seemed to grow louder. More insistent. "Mickey, go shut up your dog."

No reply. *That's odd.* Usually, Mickey was a light sleeper. Gina was surprised he hadn't gotten up to check on the dog. She rolled over to look at Mickey. The side of the bed was empty. *Oh, I guess he has gone down to check on Blaze after all.* She rolled back over and tried to go back to sleep.

A few minutes passed. *If Mickey went down to quiet the dog, why is she still making such a racket?* Gina sat up and took a sip of water from a glass on her nightstand. It looked as though she'd have to stop the dog from barking herself. She pulled on her fuzzy white robe and approached the top of the staircase.

"Be quiet," she chastised Blaze.

In response, Blaze began howling even louder. She raced into the kitchen and then rushed back to the base of the stairs as if to implore, "Follow me."

Gina's left knee had been bothering her of late. She gripped the handrail as she made her way downstairs. Her knee seemed stiffest when she first got out of bed.

"What are you so worked up about, Blaze?"

She followed Blaze into the kitchen and turned up the lights. Her eyes were immediately drawn to the middle of the kitchen, near the island. She spotted Mickey lying face down, motionless. She stifled a scream and rushed to his side.

"Mickey, what happened? Are you okay?"

"No, I fell, and I'm paralyzed. I can't move at all. You need to call for an ambulance."

Gina attempted to suppress the panic rising within her. "Okay, but my phone is upstairs. I'll go get it."

"You can use mine. It's on the counter," Mickey said. "Please hurry. I'm not sure how long I've been here. I feel terrible, and I'm in a lot of pain. It's getting harder to breathe."

With shaking hands, Gina grabbed Mickey's phone and dialed 911. "I need an ambulance at 93 Worcester Place. My husband is lying on our kitchen floor. He fell, and now he's paralyzed…"

. . . .

DISPATCHER: "Request for first aid at 93 Worcester Place for a 52-year-old male fall victim who is unable to move."

We have assigned crew nights from 10:00 p.m. to 6:00 a.m. Tonight was my crew night. I rolled out of bed and joined Archie Harris and Mason Chapman at the first aid building. A few minutes later, our ambulance pulled up in front of a two-story beige stucco house. I rang the doorbell while simultaneously turning the doorknob. Several dogs began barking, announcing our arrival. I pushed the door open, and we stepped inside. We passed through a living room, where a beagle and shepherd watched us with interest.

When I entered the kitchen, I spotted a third dog—this one brown and white—lying next to our patient. A pajama-clad, middle-aged man lay facedown on the tile floor.

"I wish I could give you a giant bone right now, old girl," he said.

A woman wearing a worried expression stood near him. "I'm Gina Davis, and this is my husband, Mickey. He's had a terrible fall."

"Hi. I'm Andrea, and this is Mason and Archie. We're EMTs on the Pine Cove First Aid Squad. I see you have someone guarding you."

"Blaze saved my life," Mickey said. "I'm not sure how much longer I could have lasted like this. She woke up my wife."

I gave Blaze a quick pat on the head. "A four-legged guardian angel."

"You can say that again," Mickey agreed. "Gina, you better move Blaze out of the way so they can help me. Please give her an extra treat from me."

Gina took hold of Blaze by the collar and gently pulled her back. "I'll put her in the living room with the other two."

I knelt by Mickey's head. "I'm going to put my hands on either side of your head to keep it still."

Mason knelt on Mickey's left side. "Are you having trouble breathing?"

"Yes, a little," Mickey replied.

Archie turned on our portable oxygen tank to 15 liters per minute and handed Mason a non-rebreather mask, which he slipped onto Mickey's face.

"Do you have any pain?" Mason asked.

Mickey winced. "Yes, my neck hurts. And I can't move my arms or legs."

"We're going to take you to Bakersville Hospital," Mason said. "It's a trauma center, so they'll be able to help you."

He ran his fingers along Mickey's spine to check for pain and obvious deformity.

Archie placed a backboard directly alongside Mickey. "We're going to roll you from your stomach directly onto a backboard, which will keep your spine from moving."

We rolled Mickey onto his back, and then Archie put a cervical collar around his neck to keep it stable.

Mason placed a blood-pressure cuff around Mickey's left upper arm and pumped it up. "The BP is 90 over 62, and the pulse is 84, strong and regular. His respiratory rate is 22 and shallow. His pulse ox is 92 percent before oxygen. It's up to 97 percent now."

Mason did a thorough head-to-toe examination, noting bruising on Mickey's chin.

"Can you feel me touch you?" he asked, touching various spots on Mickey's arms and legs.

Mickey closed his eyes, deep in concentration. "I think I can feel you touch my legs but not my arms. Do you think I'm going to be okay?"

"First, the trauma doctor will assess you to see what's causing the problem. For example, they'll see if you broke anything when you fell. Once they determine the problem, then they can figure out the best way to help you."

"I think I must have hit my chest first because it knocked out the popcorn I was choking on," Mickey said.

"It's amazing that it came out when you fell," Archie said.

Together, we lifted the backboard, moving Mickey from the floor to the stretcher.

. . . .

The next few minutes passed in a blur for Mickey. He watched his kitchen ceiling disappear from view as the EMTs rolled him outside. As the stretcher bumped along his gravel driveway, he looked up toward the sky (the only direction he could look with his head strapped down) and prayed for a miracle.

God, You got the popcorn out of my throat, and You helped Blaze alert Gina to help me. Now, please let me be able to move my arms and legs again. One bright star seemed to twinkle in response. Or maybe it was just his wishful thinking. Mickey didn't have time to ponder it before being lifted into the ambulance.

. . . .

Archie checked to make sure the stretcher was securely locked in place. "I'll be your driver today, and Mason and Andrea will keep you company back here. Gina will sit up front with me. We'll be there before you know it."

"Thank you," Mickey said.

Bakersville Hospital was about 15 minutes away. A few minutes into the trip, Mason rechecked Mickey's vital signs. "How's your breathing?" he asked.

Mickey inhaled as deeply as he could. "Better with the oxygen."

"That's good. I know I asked you briefly in the home about your medical history, but I'm going to ask you in more detail now so I can type the information into my laptop."

Mickey was glad for the questions because they helped distract him from his pain and worry about not being able to move.

"I have diabetes and high blood pressure. With all that's going on, I wouldn't be surprised if my sugar's off. Last year, I had a heart attack and needed a stent. My neck was bothering me even before I fell tonight, but I hadn't gone to the doctor about it yet."

"They'll check your glucose level in the hospital to make sure it's okay. Are you on any medications?" I asked.

Mickey rattled off a bunch. "And I'm allergic to penicillin."

I switched Mickey's oxygen from the onboard tank back to the portable one. "We're pulling into the parking garage now. In a minute, the entire trauma team will be helping you."

"Thanks for everything," Mickey said. He prayed God hadn't saved him from choking only to spend the rest of his days as a quadriplegic.

. . . .

Mickey woke from a restless sleep when Gina tapped his arm. The emergency department stretcher was not conducive to getting any shut-eye, even though he was exhausted from the entire ordeal. Not to mention terrified of the prospect of never walking again.

When Mickey first arrived, Dr. Rodriguez, nurses, and techs worked on him. They started an IV line, inspected him all over, and sent him to a battery of tests that scanned every part of his body: brain, chest, spine, and extremities. He'd finally drifted off to sleep what felt like only a few minutes ago.

Gina stroked Mickey's head. "Honey, Dr. Rodriguez is here to speak to you."

Mickey realized he wasn't on a spinal immobilization board anymore. Instead, he wore a special cervical collar, and the head of his stretcher was elevated about 30 degrees. He appreciated that he could see more than just the ceiling tiles.

Dr. Rodriguez cleared his throat. "The good news is that you got here relatively quickly. Time is of the essence with spinal cord injuries. And your history of diabetes and heart problems increases that urgency."

"I have my dog Blaze to thank for that."

"Your wife filled me in on what happened. That dog sounds like a real keeper," Dr. Rodriguez said.

"She sure is," Mickey replied.

I tried to say no to Jimmy Hudson. I didn't want a third dog, even if it was going to be only temporary. Yet while my own canines went off to sleep, the dog I didn't want saved my life. The dog I tried to turn away turned out to be my guardian angel.

Dr. Rodriguez took a step closer to Mickey. "I have some of your test results back. As you may have guessed, the fall injured your spinal cord. It caused what we call cervical cord compression. That means the spinal cord in the region of your neck is getting squeezed, causing pain, numbness, and weakness."

"Is the paralysis permanent?" Mickey asked. He steeled himself for the answer.

Dr. Rodriguez paused before answering. "I certainly hope not. But you need emergency surgery. The neurosurgeon is reviewing your films now, including your X-rays and CT scan of your spine. We'll begin prepping you shortly for the operation if you're in agreement."

Mickey blinked rapidly. "Yes, of course, please do whatever you think is best. I want to walk again."

"Absolutely. We want that too."

"The pain is so bad. It's shooting from my neck into my shoulders," Mickey said.

"We can adjust your pain medications to give you some relief. Do you have any questions? If not, I'll see you later today, after your surgery."

"No, I think you answered all of them. Thank you for all your help."

After Dr. Rodriguez left the room, the events of the long day replayed in Mickey's head. As horrible a situation as he was in right now, he felt fortunate in a way. He'd fallen just the right way to dislodge the popcorn from his throat. Otherwise, he'd be long dead already. Through the persistent heroic actions of Blaze, he'd gotten to the hospital quicky enough to give him a chance of recovery with emergency surgery. He fervently prayed God and his guardian angel would stay by his side during the next critical hours.

. . . .

Three months later

As I walked around Weeping Willow Lake, I paused to pet a large brown-and-white dog who was walking with his owner. The dog looked familiar, but I couldn't place him. I looked up from petting him and glanced at his owner. With a start, I realized it was Mickey, our patient who'd fallen months ago in his kitchen. He was walking with the assistance of a single-point cane. The dog with him was Blaze.

"Wow, you look great!" I exclaimed and reintroduced myself. I didn't expect him to recognize me from that traumatic day.

"I can't thank you and your squad enough for helping me. The doc says I'm doing even better than they could have hoped. I'm allowed to start physical therapy soon." Mickey fished a crumpled piece of paper out of his pocket and handed it to me to read.

I unfolded the paper and realized it was a physical therapy prescription: "Cervical cord compression with traumatic cervical cord syndrome s/p anterior cervical discectomy, fusion C4-5 and C5-C6, and cervical spine allograft." In other words, his spinal cord in his neck had been compressed as a result of trauma. The spinal surgeon operated on one of the cervical discs and fused the bones together at two levels.

"Wow, that's a very serious surgery," I said. "It must have been an amazing success, since you're walking with just a cane."

"It sure was. I spent three months in a rehab hospital that specializes in spinal cord injuries. First, I started by taking a few steps in the parallel bars. After a month, I could walk short distances with a rolling walker. I'm making an unbelievable recovery." Mickey pointed upwards. "I have the big guy upstairs to thank."

I scratched Blaze's ear. "And if I recall correctly, a dog named Blaze. Is your friend going to take him back?"

A big smile lit Mickey's face. "No way. He's our dog now!"

Chapter 15

Our Father

*And without faith it is impossible to please God, because
anyone who comes to him must believe that he exists
and that he rewards those who earnestly seek him.*

HEBREWS 11:6

Sweat dripped down Simon Wickerton's cheeks and along the nape of his neck. It ran in a steady stream from his forehead into his eyes. In fact, perspiration ran in rivers along his entire body. He swiped at his eyes, trying to wipe the sweat from his eyelids.

When he started this run a half hour ago, his goal was to run along the boardwalk. Maybe a cooling sea breeze would relieve the unrelenting August heat. It took a half hour to jog here from his house, and now he wondered if he should have taken his car. There was barely a breeze stirring here, and he'd still have to run all the way home after his jaunt along the boardwalk.

He looked across Ocean Boulevard at the dunes that beckoned him. Although no breeze stirred on this side of the street, he hoped he'd find one closer to the ocean. Heck, he'd run on the sand along the water's edge if that's what it took to cool off. Maybe he could even take a quick dip.

With eyes focused on the boardwalk, Simon rushed into the intersection. He grunted when an unexpected impact launched him off his feet high into the air. A wave of crippling pain swept over his body before his mind succumbed to darkness.

. . . .

Juan Chaverro could scarcely believe his eyes. A runner on the west side of Ocean Boulevard darted into traffic, never stopping or looking to make sure it was safe to cross. A dark-colored SUV sped directly toward the runner. Juan cringed in anticipation of the impact. He watched as the victim sailed through the air before landing in the middle of the hot asphalt road. Juan flipped on his hazards and threw his gearshift into park. He knew a little about first aid. Maybe he could help.

Heart pounding at the sight of the motionless man, Juan took a deep breath before kneeling next to him. He checked for a carotid pulse. *No pulse!* He noticed a young woman holding a cell phone drawing closer.

"Call 911!" he yelled. He placed his hands on the center of the man's chest and began chest compressions.

(Hands-only CPR means performing chest compressions without mouth-to-mouth breathing. It allows for early bystander intervention without fear of getting exposed to possible infectious materials from unprotected ventilations. According to the American Heart Association, hands-only CPR is as effective as traditional CPR in the first several minutes following a patient's cardiac arrest.)

After about 30 compressions, the man stirred slightly but didn't open his eyes. Juan paused and checked again for a pulse. Now he felt a strong pulse beating at the side of the man's neck. However, his eyes remained closed.

Juan tapped his shoulder. "Wake up! Can you hear me?" *No response.*

DISPATCHER: "Request for first aid in the 300 block of Ocean Boulevard for a pedestrian struck by a motor vehicle."

Within a few minutes, Buddy Stone, Archie Harris, Jessie Barnes, and I arrived on scene with the ambulance. Two Pine Cove patrol cars blocked traffic. A small crowd of bystanders surrounded a man who lay flat on his back in the middle of the road. Officer Vinnie McGovern stood close to the victim, speaking on his portable radio with dispatch. I could hear him working on trying to identify our patient.

A young man knelt next to our patient. He turned eagerly toward us as we drew closer.

"I saw the whole thing," he said. "This man jogged out into the road and got waffled by an SUV. He didn't have a pulse at first. I'm certified in CPR, and I did hands-only for about a minute before he got his pulse back and started breathing on his own. He was unconscious for about two minutes, but now he's beginning to come around."

Officer McGovern returned his radio to its holster and stepped closer. "I just got a positive ID on him. His name is Simon Wickerton. He lives in Marina Beach."

Simon's eyes popped open. He gazed at us and frowned. "Who are all of you? What happened?"

"We're members of the Pine Cove First Aid Squad," Archie said. "You've had an accident. You were struck by an SUV while crossing the street. Do you remember anything that happened before you were hit?"

Simon shook his head. "No. I mean, let me think. I'm not sure. I remember leaving my house to go for a jog, but it's fuzzy after that."

Simon lived about three miles from the accident site, so the fact that he was amnesic about the events leading up to the accident was a sign of head trauma, such as a concussion or worse, a brain bleed.

"I'm fine," he said. "I don't need to go to the hospital."

"Let's start by checking you from head to toe," I said, kneeling next to him.

He had lacerations on his left elbow and knee and road rash across his back. There wasn't any heavy bleeding or obvious bony deformities, but I was concerned by his initial loss of consciousness and current level of awareness and insight into his situation, not to mention his lack of heartbeat when first found by the bystander. His blood pressure, heart rate, and pulse ox were all within normal parameters. However, this could change if he was experiencing internal bleeding. Due to the mechanism of injury, I knew Simon should go to the hospital to get checked out.

"The doctor in the emergency department can perform X-rays and CT scans that we can't do here in the field," I said.

"Thanks, but no. I'm good. Anyway, hospitals have germs. I don't want to pick up any illnesses."

I asked Simon his name, the date, and where he was. He knew his name, but he wasn't sure about the day or location. We'd already determined he was amnesic to the event. Our crew had no intention of taking no for an answer. Since he wasn't mentally sound at this moment, we'd transport him to the hospital.

Buddy placed a cervical collar on Simon, and we rolled him onto a backboard. As we loaded him into the ambulance, paramedics Ty Fleming and Paula Pritchard met us. After assessing Simon, Paula activated the hospital's trauma team. That way, they'd be ready and waiting for us.

"This is overkill. I'm fine. I really could have just jogged home. Now, I'll be sitting in the ER all night," Simon grumbled. "I have better things to do."

"You're health comes first," Paula said. "It's our responsibility to make sure you're okay."

The rest of the trip passed quickly, and soon we were met at the ED entrance by a team of highly specialized caregivers who ushered us into the trauma bay. As Paula gave the report to the trauma physician, our squad members shifted Simon from our stretcher to the hospital's. He seemed overall as if he was improving, but I knew he was in the right place. Letting him sign off RMA (refusing medical advice) would have been a big mistake.

We returned to the ambulance and headed back to Pine Cove.

"I hope he's going to be okay," Buddy said.

I straightened out the linens on top of the stretcher. "I'm glad he went willingly in the end." I scarcely finished my sentence when our pagers went off again.

> **DISPATCHER:** "Request for first aid at Pennington Manor by the pool area for an unresponsive male, unknown if breathing at this time."

Archie Harris, our driver, flipped on the overhead emergency lights. "We're responding with an ETA of about five minutes," he notified dispatch.

My mind raced with possibilities. The victim was located near a swimming pool. Could the call be water related? Or was he simply having a drink or a bite to eat at the poolside bar? I jotted the date and time of dispatch at the top of our run sheet as well as the nature of the call.

Buddy slipped on a pair of medical gloves. "Back-to-back calls with serious natures. Hopefully, this guy will snap out of it."

> **DISPATCHER:** "Update on call at Pennington Manor. Patient was unconscious but is now conscious."

Archie parked the rig in front of the manor, and we scrambled out. An older woman with snow-white hair wearing a knee-length floral dress stood waiting for us.

"He's around back. Follow me." She led us along a brick pathway around the outside of the building to the rear area, near the pool and bar. Tall arborvitae lent privacy to the pretty alcove, and beds of impatiens added to the beauty. Patrons filled about a dozen tables surrounding the far side of the pool. Our patient sat at one of the tables in the middle.

Officer Vinnie McGovern bent over an older gentleman, who sat slouched in his chair, a large brown-and-white striped umbrella providing some much-needed shade. Although the sun was setting, it was still high enough to suffuse the area in heat. I could see why some of the visitors here today might have been attracted to the idea of taking a dip to cool off.

"This is George Pudinski. He's 70," Officer McGovern told us.

"Thanks for coming," George said. "I think I'm starting to feel a little better now."

His appearance didn't completely match his words. Blue eyes shone brightly in an unnaturally pale face. Perspiration glistened on his face and soaked his shirt. Even though he hadn't been in the pool, he looked as if he had.

Officer McGovern adjusted the umbrella so that it better protected George from the sun's rays. "He was out cold when I got here but came around after a minute."

"I think I may have overdone it in the heat today. I walked three miles earlier this afternoon," George said.

"Have you been drinking fluids today?" I asked. Lack of proper hydration is often a contributing factor with our heat-related first aid calls.

"Yes, some. I had about four cups of water." George glanced at his place setting. "And two glasses of wine."

The long walk in the hot sun coupled with several glasses of wine probably caused dehydration, leading to George's syncopal episode. However, he'd need a checkup at the hospital to confirm if his medical problem was indeed heat related. They could do an EKG to rule out possible cardiac or other causes for the fainting spell.

I squatted next to him and felt his radial pulse. "His heart rate is 58 and regular." I placed a blood-pressure cuff around his upper arm. I suspected it would be low, but it was *really* low. I couldn't hear it with a stethoscope, so I had to check it by palpation. When you take a blood pressure by palpation, you only get a systolic (top) number. "His BP is 88 by palp."

"Let's get him lying down and on some oxygen," Jessie suggested.

We gently lowered George onto the ground. Archie placed an oxygen non-rebreather mask over his nose and mouth, setting the gauge to 15 liters per minute.

"How are you feeling now?" I asked, reinflating the BP cuff so I could recheck his pressure.

"I'm definitely not right yet," George said. "I'm feeling kind of dizzy, but a little better now that I'm lying down." His blood pressure increased to 94 palp, still awfully low.

Just then, paramedics Paula Pritchard and Ty Fleming arrived. Archie briefed them on George's status.

"Let's get him on the stretcher, and we'll do a full assessment in the rig," Ty said. "It sounds like he needs some IV fluids."

As a team, we lifted George from the ground onto our stretcher and rolled him back along the brick path to our ambulance. George remained pasty white, though perhaps a smidgeon better than when we first arrived. I noticed a middle-aged gentleman wearing a polo shirt and khakis following behind us at a respectful distance. As we loaded George into the ambulance, he caught up to us and tapped my shoulder.

"Hi, my name is Father Patrick. I'm a priest. Could you please ask your patient if he would like me to say a prayer?"

"Thank you so much. Absolutely." I stepped into the ambulance and asked George if he'd be okay with the priest's suggestion.

George nodded. "That would be terrific. I could definitely use some prayers right now."

"Just give me a few minutes to finish my assessment and start the IV," Ty said as he attached EKG electrodes to George's chest.

I relayed the message to Father Patrick, and a few minutes later, I escorted him into the back of our ambulance. Jessie paused from writing the report, and Buddy finished switching George from a non-rebreather mask to a simple nasal cannula.

George held up his hand in greeting. "Thanks so much."

Father Patrick stood over George, praying quietly. I caught some of the words and could see from George's face that he found comfort in them. After finishing, Father Patrick asked, "Would you like to say the Our Father?"

I recognized the look of panic that flashed across George's face and could tell he feared he might not correctly recall the words to the Lord's Prayer.

"Let's say it together," I suggested.

"That would be terrific," George said, his relief almost palpable.

Then George, Father Patrick, Jessie, Ty, Buddy, and I solemnly recited the prayer together. In that moment, I felt the Lord's presence. *A perfect God moment.*

"Bless all of you and thank you for all you do," George said. He shook hands with Father Patrick, and soon we were on our way to the emergency room. The fluids from the IV line dripped into his veins, helping to rehydrate him. By the time we arrived at the hospital, he declared he felt 95 percent better.

After the call, as we were cleaning our stretcher, Paula came to update us on the condition of Simon Wickerton, the patient we'd brought into trauma right before the call for George.

"I just spoke to the trauma nurse," Paula said. "Simon has a brain bleed and five rib fractures."

Thank goodness we transported Simon to the hospital in a timely manner so he could receive the critical care he needed.

God our Father was taking care of His followers in their time of need.

Chapter 16

Not on My Watch

"Do not let your hearts be troubled and do not be afraid."

JOHN 14:27

love all of God's creatures, but I love some more than others. Take squirrels, for example. They're okay, I guess. I think they're better from a distance than up close. Some of the ones that live around me are bold, fearless, and apparently hungry. I'll admit I'm a bit scared of them. The ones that live in one of our local parks will S-T-A-L-K you if you have any food. When I visited the park with my children when they were toddlers, naturally I brought snacks. I made sure to keep them well hidden. They had to be in a bag heavy enough that a squirrel couldn't drag it away. I've seen them run off with entire lunch bags.

If you keep the snacks in a large bag, like a backpack, it's crucial to keep it fully zipped. Otherwise, you can kiss your mini-pretzels and cookies goodbye. Once you decide it's time to eat the snacks, the word *vigilance* takes on a whole new meaning. I pull the goodies out of my bag as discreetly as possible. No matter, though. When I look up, numerous sets of brown eyes stare at me intently, their little bodies inching closer and closer. I've seen them jump directly onto people's arms and grab the food clean out of their hands. I've witnessed them climbing straight up an unsuspecting person's leg. Natural response? Scream and throw food. Score a victory point for the squirrel.

My next-door neighbor hand-feeds squirrels peanuts each day. Usually, they stick around her house just in case she happens to come outside with a handful of treats. However, they occasionally wander into our yard. Usually, I don't have food on me, so they leave me alone. However, if I go to visit my neighbor, they surround me, determined to discover if I have any nuts. (I assure you and them, I don't.)

One warm spring morning, I stood in front of the garage with my husband, Rick, preparing to do some gardening. Our house is set back from the road, allowing for an expansive front lawn. About 40 feet away, closer to the street, a small brown squirrel lounged on our sunny grass. He was enjoying the beautiful day and was far enough from me (i.e., not stalking me for food) that I didn't mind his presence.

Just as I glanced down to don a pair of gardening gloves, Rick glanced up. "Uh-oh, a hawk."

My head jerked upwards, just in time to see the large red-tailed hawk making a beeline for the squirrel. "No!" I hollered, taking off at a sprint. I rushed along the driveway, waving my arms up and down like a lunatic and continuing my verbal onslaught to discourage the hawk from making my neighbor's semi-domesticated squirrel his next meal. Not on my watch!

DISPATCHER: "Request for first aid for an assault victim. Expedite — patient is in imminent danger."

Of course, my pager didn't really go off. But I bet the squirrel wished it had.

I arrived a shade too late. The hawk did what it's born to do, what nature calls it to do. It grabbed hold of the writhing squirrel. I bit back a wave of nausea. I don't like watching television programs about wildlife survival (i.e., animals eating other animals). Seeing it happen right in front of your face is a thousand times worse.

Should I be trying to interfere with nature? I don't know. Maybe not. At the time, my instincts as a volunteer first aid squad member kicked in automatically. It didn't matter that I don't really like squirrels. I just knew this one needed help. So, I gave it my best shot.

The hawk flew across our front lawn, the squirrel dangling from its claws. I rushed closer, frantically waving my arms. "Let it go!" The hawk continued its flight, now at the level of my head. I'd never be able to catch it now. It gained height, soaring out of reach.

Something fell from the sky and landed at my feet with a small thud. The squirrel! Was he dead? At first glance, it was hard to tell. It didn't look promising. He looked pretty roughed up and wasn't moving at all. I glanced up to make sure the hawk wasn't coming back to reclaim his prize.

Rick arrived next to me, holding a large stick. He poked the squirrel gently. *No response.* Had the hawk's massive claws punctured a vital organ? I knelt next to the squirrel, studying his chest closely. "He's breathing!"

We both stood watch over him for several long minutes, giving him a chance to recover without the hawk circling back to finish what he'd started. After a minute or so, the squirrel's eyes popped open. He eyed us warily, then hopped away and took cover under one of our large evergreen bushes. Mission "Save the Squirrel" was a success, and I didn't even have to touch it (thank goodness).

. . . .

Are there any little animals other than squirrels that make me nervous? *Yes.*

One day, I was traveling along back roads toward the first aid building when something in the middle of the road caught my eye. It looked like a decorative porcelain bowl. Why would someone leave that in the middle of the road?

As I drew closer, I realized the small "bowl" was slowly moving. *Very slowly moving.* I gasped. A turtle! I've mostly only seen turtles in the zoo or protected areas. I'd never seen one in our neighborhood, and most certainly not crossing a road. If I didn't do something to help, I feared it would become roadkill. Not on my watch.

> **DISPATCHER:** "Request for first aid for a patient who needs assistance crossing the road."

In reality, my pager remained silent. I was on my own for this one. I shifted from drive into park and flipped on my hazard lights before striding over to the reptile. His green-and-orange shell looked to be about ten inches in diameter. I could just pick him up and deposit him safely in the bushes at the side of the road. Except...I was afraid to touch him. What if he snapped? What if he tried to bite me? I don't know much about turtles except I've heard that once there was this race and the tortoise beat the hare.

Think, think, think. What could I do? *A towel!* That's it. I had an old beach towel in my trunk. I could use that to scoop up the turtle. I popped my trunk and pulled it out. A car zipped past going the other direction, slowing down just enough to give me a curious look. I guess they didn't notice the turtle. I'm glad this road isn't particularly busy. But I couldn't block this lane all day. I needed to move the animal and get on my way.

Clutching the towel, I drew closer to the turtle. Sensing my presence, he withdrew his head into his shell. I began having second thoughts. *What if the turtle bites me through this thin towel? What if he pokes his head out again, and it whips around and clamps down on my hand?* I needed an infusion of bravery. I hovered uncertainly over the turtle, drawing closer but then pulling back. *If only I could just grab it.*

I'm embarrassed to say, this went on probably for a full five minutes before I was able to muster up the courage to act. I folded the towel several times to make it thicker. I held my breath, swooped in, grabbed the turtle, then half-ran to the side of the road where I gently placed him into the bushes facing *away* from the road. His head stayed in the whole time. He never tried to bite me, thank goodness. I like turtles, but I prefer looking at them rather than touching them. I'm glad I had the opportunity to help one of God's creatures.

. . . .

Perhaps little occurrences like the ones above are preparing us to act when the stakes are higher—as when a person desperately needs assistance.

My children and I spent Labor Day morning squeezing out the last bit of summer at the pool and beach. By lunchtime, we said good-bye to summer and turned our thoughts to preparing for the return to school. On our way home, we chatted about this year's classes and teachers. When I approached the railroad crossing closest to the train station, I slowed to a stop as the gates came down in front of my car. I didn't see a train yet but knew it would arrive shortly.

My attention turned to a very elderly woman who was walking s-l-o-w-l-y across the tracks, heading from east to west. Or west to east? I looked more closely. As a physical therapist, I tend to analyze everyone's gait who walks by me. It comes as naturally as breathing. If you have a foot drop or a limp, I'm probably going to notice. This woman appeared to be trying to go in a westward direction, but backwards! *Why is she walking backwards? Doesn't she realize a train is coming? Why doesn't she hurry up?*

With burgeoning horror, I realized why she was facing the wrong direction as she tried to walk. The front wheels of her rolling walker were stuck in between the ruts of the railroad tracks, and she was trying to pull it loose. I figured she probably couldn't walk without it. If she abandoned the walker and fell on the tracks…

I sucked in my breath and thrust open my driver's side door, not wasting time by saying anything to my children. I didn't have to. As young as they were, they too realized what was happening.

I began sprinting toward her, a plan formulating in my head. I would yank on the walker once. If I couldn't dislodge it, I would carry or drag her off the tracks. That is, if the train wasn't already on top of us.

The distant whistle of an approaching train drew closer, louder, scarier. *Impending doom.* Everything was happening too fast. If I could just stop time for a minute, I could free the woman's walker and escort her to safety. Although I couldn't stop time, I could pray. I sent a silent prayer to heaven. *Help, God!*

I glanced to the left as I rushed toward the woman. A large black monster approached, heading toward the station. In that instant, the walker pulled loose. The woman wasted no time backing the rest of the way off the tracks. I feared the whooshing air from the train could knock her over, perhaps even suck her underneath the train, if she didn't get far enough out of the way.

The squeal of brakes sounded downright divine. The train came to a stop a mere 15 feet from where the woman had stood just seconds ago. As I watched her slowly turn her walker and amble away, I was filled with profound relief. I'm not sure I breathed until that moment. Now, my lungs filled with the sweet air of averted disaster. My arms and legs shook slightly as I turned back toward my car.

A middle-aged man wearing dark sunglasses approached me. "Are you okay? Is she okay? I saw you jump out of your car, and I knew right away something must be wrong."

I nodded. "Her walker wheel was stuck in the railroad ties, but it came out just in the nick of time."

Another gentleman approached from the train station parking lot. "I saw everything that was happening, but I was too far away to help. Thank God it turned out okay."

Thank God, indeed. That woman's guardian angel must have worked hard to pull off that miracle. I probably gave my own guardian angel a good scare too.

By the time I got back into my car and crossed over the tracks, I spotted the woman slowly walking along the sidewalk. She didn't look any the worse for wear, despite the near accident. I sent a brief after-prayer up to heaven.

Thank You, God.

Chapter 17

Wings to Fly

But those who hope in the LORD
will renew their strength.
They will soar on wings like eagles.

ISAIAH 40:31

Early April

DISPATCHER: "Request for first aid at 302 Bergen Street for a 28-year-old female who passed out, now conscious and alert."

Jessie Barnes, Greg Turner, Colleen Harper, and I were restocking the ambulance after returning from an earlier call. An older woman had tripped on a small throw rug, falling hard onto her right knee. We applied a cold pack, splinted her leg, and transported her to the hospital without complications. Now, it appeared that we'd be heading off to another emergency call.

Greg, a retired electrical engineer, uses his analytical brain to problem solve on rescue calls. "I'll drive," he said.

Jessie hopped into the front passenger seat. "I'll be your copilot."

"Hopefully, this call will be quick. I have to take my dog to the groomer in an hour," Colleen said. She and I were already in the back of the rig, organizing the overhead cabinets. We took a seat, buckled up, and Greg called us in service.

Within a few minutes, Greg pulled up in front of a red brick Colonial. A pair of old sycamore trees shaded much of the front yard. Spring flowers bursting with vibrant purples, pinks, and blues lined the concrete walkway. We found our patient, a young woman with long dark hair who looked to be in her late twenties, sitting in a white wicker chair on the front porch.

"Hi, I'm so sorry to trouble you," she said. "I'm fine, really. I don't need any medical help. I passed out for a few seconds, but I'm okay now."

"Hi, I'm Jessie with the Pine Cove First Aid Squad. Is it okay if we ask you a few questions and check you over?"

"Sure, that would be great. But I don't want to go to the hospital or anything."

"Okay. What's your name?" Jessie asked, pulling a stethoscope and blood-pressure cuff out of our first aid kit.

"Ruth Zimmerman," she said, leaning back in the chair. "I don't have any medical problems that I know of."

"Do you take any medications? Are you allergic to any that you know of?" I asked.

"No, I'm pretty healthy," Ruth said. "I passed out once in the shower, about a year ago. I think I was dehydrated. And today, I haven't eaten breakfast yet."

I paused from taking notes in our notepad. "Did you fall when you passed out?"

"No, fortunately, I was sitting in a chair. One second, I felt okay, but then everything went dark. When I came around, I was slumped over on the table."

"Well, your blood pressure and pulse are normal," Jessie said. "We recommend you go get checked out at the hospital, especially since it's not your first time passing out."

"Thanks, but no. I think I'm fine. I'll call my friend Carol to come over and stay with me for a bit. She lives next door." Ruth gestured toward the corner property just to the east of her own house.

I prepared the paperwork for her to sign a refusal of medical advice (RMA). After she signed it, Colleen also signed it as a witness.

"Please call us back if you don't feel well or if it happens again," Greg said.

"Thanks again," Ruth said, rising to her feet. "I feel much better. Nothing that a little breakfast won't fix."

We packed up and headed back to our building. Colleen glanced at her watch and smiled. "Still on time for the dog groomer."

. . . .

One month later

"I can't wait for Daisy's wedding. I can't believe it's only three weeks away," Ruth said, eyes half closed as she enjoyed floating on a raft in her neighbor's pool.

The early May sun's rays were surprisingly strong. Carol Sharkey dunked her head under water to cool off and then resurfaced. "Me too. I'm so happy for her. She finally found her Mr. Right."

Ruth sighed. "Now if only we'd be so lucky and find our Mr. Right."

Carol giggled. "You know what they say. Always a bridesmaid, never a bride."

Ruth splashed water at her. "Ha-ha. Just wait and see. One day, we'll find him."

They lapsed into a comfortable silence, soaking up the sun's rays.

. . . .

The warm sun suffused my backyard with bright light. I coaxed our Belgian shepherd, Montana, to do her "business." When my pager went off, I grabbed her collar and hustled her inside.

DISPATCHER: "Request for first aid at 300 Bergen Street for an unresponsive female. Patient is in the backyard, next to the pool. Unknown if patient is breathing at this time."

I slipped on a pair of canvas sneakers and rushed to my car, calling out, "I'm going on a first aid call," just in case anyone in my family was listening. As I drove toward the building, we were redispatched.

DISPATCHER: "Request for first aid at 300 Bergen Street for an unresponsive female. Update: CPR in progress. Park on the east side of the house and enter backyard through the rear gate."

Jessie was already in the driver's seat and Colleen in the passenger seat when I arrived at the first aid building. I yanked open the rear door and joined Greg, who was busy pulling the defibrillator out of the cabinet to prepare for the call. When a person's heart stops, every second counts.

"We're in service," Jessie said, pressing hard on the accelerator. I grabbed onto an overhead bar to steady myself as I pulled the portable suction unit off its shelf.

Once I was sitting on the ambulance bench, Greg tossed me a pair of medical gloves. "I've got the defibrillator and the first aid bag," he said.

"This is right next to the house where we had the call for the young woman who passed out last month," I noted, pulling on the gloves.

"That's right, the RMA," Greg said. "I think her name was Ruth."

Jessie parked behind a patrol car along the side of a large corner property. Majestic oak trees shaded a century-old Victorian with a beautiful wraparound porch. "We're on location," Jessie notified dispatch.

As I yanked open the gate to the backyard, I could see Officer Pedro Suarez and Officer Brad Sims performing CPR on a young woman. As I grew closer, I realized with dismay the victim was indeed Ruth, the young woman who lived next door to this house. A petite young woman in a black-and-white bikini stood close by.

Officer Sims glanced up from performing chest compressions. "This is Ruth Zimmerman. She was swimming in her neighbor Carol

Sharkey's pool. Carol said Ruth got out of the pool and suddenly collapsed. She tried to rouse her but couldn't, so she called 911."

"So, it's not a near-drowning?" Greg asked.

"No, Ruth wasn't in distress or complaining of anything when she climbed out of the pool," Officer Sims replied.

After Officer Sims completed a set of 30 compressions, Officer Suarez squeezed the bag valve mask twice, taking care to make sure Ruth's airway was open.

"I was working a traffic detail just one block from here, so I got here fast," Officer Suarez said. "I shocked once with the defibrillator, but we didn't get back pulses."

I knelt next to Officer Suarez and took over holding the mask in place over the lower half of Ruth's face. She scarcely looked like the woman I met four weeks ago. That woman exuded vitality. This person appeared gray and lifeless. I suppressed a shudder and concentrated on trying to resuscitate her. Liquid slid from the corner of her mouth.

"We need suction."

"Got it," Jessie said, threading a rigid Yankauer catheter into Ruth's mouth. Using a figure-eight pattern, he sucked out the fluid.

"The defibrillator is analyzing again. Stand clear," Officer Sims directed. The machine revved up, building energy for a shock. I held my breath as he pressed the shock button.

After shocking Ruth, Officer Suarez placed his index and middle finger along the groove at the side of her neck. "I feel a carotid pulse."

We resumed rescue breaths, one every five seconds. Liquid bubbled from the corner of Ruth's mouth again.

"We need more suction," I said. Jessie quickly removed the fluid.

I glanced up and noticed that Colleen was gathering information from Ruth's friend Carol. The two stood at the poolside. I strained to hear their conversation.

"Can you tell me exactly what happened this morning?" Colleen asked.

"Ruth came over for a dip about an hour ago, which she often does. We've lived next door to each other since we were kids. Everything seemed fine. We chatted about this and that. She never said anything about not feeling good. She just said she felt like it was time to get out, and she wanted to use the bathroom."

"We had a first aid call for Ruth a month ago when she passed out at her house. Do you know if she ever followed up with her doctor?" Colleen asked.

A tear slid down Carol's cheek. She wiped it away. "Not that I know of. At least, she didn't tell me she did."

"Do you know if your friend takes any medications?"

"She has an inhaler for exercise-induced asthma. But we weren't exercising in the pool. We were just lounging around. And she didn't say anything about feeling short of breath."

"Does she have any allergies?" Colleen asked.

"Yes, penicillin and peanuts."

"Could she have been exposed to any nuts this morning?"

Carol shook her head. "We haven't eaten anything."

I heard approaching sirens. The paramedics would be here any minute. Greg fetched the backboard from the ambulance. Before the medics arrived, we carefully rolled Ruth onto the backboard, strapped her in, placed her on the stretcher, and wheeled her to the ambulance.

"Our dispatcher made contact with Ruth's parents," Officer Sims said. "They'll meet you at the hospital. They should be there within a half hour."

Just as we were loading Ruth into the rig, paramedics Arthur Williamson and Kennisha Smythe pulled up behind us. Colleen filled them in on the situation. "We shocked once and regained a pulse, but she's still unresponsive."

As Arthur and Kennisha began assessing Ruth, I switched her oxygen from the portable tank to the onboard unit. Colleen took over squeezing the BVM. Jessie got into the driver's seat, while Greg took over the wheel of the medics' ambulance.

Kennisha placed electrodes on Ruth's chest and extremities to perform a 12-lead electrocardiogram (ECG). "She's in a normal sinus rhythm of 90 right now."

Arthur hooked up Ruth to their automatic blood-pressure cuff and placed a pulse oximeter on her left middle finger. "Her blood pressure is 92 over 64, and her pulse ox is 98 percent on 100 percent oxygen." He pulled a penlight from his breast pocket. "Her pupils are reactive to light."

Ruth began moaning. *A good sign. She's waking up.* I prepared the onboard suction unit just in case we needed it, then sat in the small side seat next to the stretcher. I felt her wrist for a radial pulse. Although it felt weak, it was definitely there. *Another good sign.* I brushed a strand of hair off her cheek, gently tucking it behind her ear.

While Kennisha checked Ruth's lung sounds, Arthur established an intravenous line in her left arm.

Ruth opened her eyes briefly, just long enough to reach toward the BVM and try to push it away with her hands.

"Ruth, it's okay," Kennisha said. "You're in an ambulance. We're taking you to the hospital."

"She's breathing pretty well on her own now. Let's switch her to a non-rebreather mask at 15 liters per minute and see how she does," Arthur said.

I pulled a non-rebreather from an overhead cabinet and hooked the end of the tubing to an oxygen port, cranking the dial to 15. Colleen removed the BVM, and I slipped the NRB mask over Ruth's mouth and nose. Meanwhile, Arthur phoned the medical director, an emergency department physician, and gave the report.

Kennisha gently stroked Ruth's shoulder. "Ruth, open your eyes."

For a few seconds, nothing. Then, Ruth slowly opened her eyes. At first, she appeared to have a dull, unfocused gaze. This slowly evolved into a look of bewilderment. She began kicking her legs and amped up her moaning.

I held her hand to try to calm her. "Ruth, your friend Carol is going to meet us at the hospital. We'll be there in a couple minutes."

She must have understood because she closed her eyes and stopped thrashing. Soon, Jessie skillfully backed our ambulance into one of the bays outside the emergency department entrance.

Veteran triage nurse Maggie Summers met us at the door. "One of you can register her and the rest take her straight down to room 5. The team is waiting for you."

Dr. Morgan, highly experienced in the field of emergency medicine, stood at the threshold of the room. Arthur filled him in on Ruth's condition. A respiratory therapist stood just outside the room with a portable mechanical ventilator, ready in case Ruth's condition deteriorated requiring her to be intubated. I prayed this wouldn't be the case.

However, despite the improvement in her condition, her situation remained touch and go. She appeared caught in a tug-of-war between heaven and Earth. Right now, Earth appeared to be gaining the advantage. *Let's hope it stays that way.*

I reflected how fortunate it was that Officer Suarez happened to be handling a traffic detail only a block away. He was able to rapidly defibrillate Ruth, and early defibrillation is key to successful resuscitations. Another case of God putting someone in the right place at the right time. After all, the traffic detail could just have easily been on the other side of town. Or he could have been tied up handling a call somewhere else.

After we moved Ruth from our stretcher to the one in room 5, Colleen and Greg went to get a replacement BVM and non-rebreather mask. Jessie and I rolled our stretcher down the hallway toward the exit. When we got closer to the door, we paused to wipe down the stretcher and put on fresh linens. Just as we were finishing, an urgent message blared over the PA system. "Code team to room 5, stat."

We paused, our eyes riveted down the hallway. Staff members rushed toward Ruth's room. My heart sank. Ruth must have lost her pulse again. Now, in the tug-of-war, perhaps heaven was gaining an advantage over Earth after all.

. . . .

After the first aid call for Ruth, I felt a jumble of emotions. Hope mixed with a heaping dose of uncertainty. It looked so promising during the ride to the hospital. Now, the ED was working feverishly to resuscitate her again. Would they succeed? The thought of such a young woman dying disheartened me, to put it mildly.

I whistled for Montana and opened the door to our backyard. I took a deep breath of cleansing fresh air, trying to let go of thoughts of Ruth and enjoy the beauty of nature. The green leaves on our maple tree rippled in the soft breeze, and I inhaled the fresh scent of daffodils and tulips. A mischievous chipmunk darted across our lawn, freezing momentarily when he spotted us, then dashing under the safety of our deck.

Montana paused underneath a towering holly tree, then began intently sniffing the ground. *Oh no. Not the frogs again.* Lately, we've had numerous frogs in our backyard, visitors from a nearby creek. I've heard licking frogs can be poisonous for dogs, so I wasn't too happy about their presence.

One thing I've learned about frogs is that you can't easily chase them away. You can't simply shoo them off. They tend to freeze in place, causing Montana to burst into a frenzied dance and excited barking. I drew closer, expecting to see a large frog.

Heavy rains from yesterday's storm soaked the earth. I held Montana's collar and peered at the muddy ground. *Yuck.* Two small dead frogs. No wonder she wasn't barking like she usually did. She must have sensed they were deceased. Flies were already landing on them. They must've been dead for a few hours or more.

I squatted to get a closer look. My attention turned to a third little creature close to the other two. I gasped. These weren't frogs! They were tiny featherless baby robins. The third one didn't have any flies on him yet. I scooped him into my hand and released Montana's collar. "Thanks for finding them, girl," I said.

My first aid instincts kicked in. I examined the robin's body closely. He looked lifeless, but...yes, there it was. An almost imperceptible rise and fall of his chest. *He's alive!*

The three baby birds must have fallen from their nest in the storm yesterday. I glanced upwards into the thick foliage of the holly tree but didn't spot a nest.

Just then, my husband, Rick, and son, John, stepped outside. Montana rushed over to greet them, and I called them over. I opened my palm to show them the tiny fluff of life.

John drew closer to examine him. "Let's call him Robin Hood."

Rick glanced upwards, but then his attention turned to the Japanese aucuba below the holly. He reached into thick foliage and pulled out a soggy, bashed up nest. "It must have blown down during the storm yesterday."

"And the baby birds must have been tossed to the ground," John added.

I cupped the survivor protectively in my hand. "It's a miracle this one is still alive."

John's gaze swept over the backyard. "I wonder where its parents are."

"Hopefully, they're close by and haven't given up yet," I said.

"I'm going to get a ladder from the garage," Rick said. "I'll see if I can figure out where the nest fell from."

"Good idea. If we can put the nest back, maybe Robin Hood's parents will find him," John said.

Rick set up our A-frame ladder and began inspecting the tree branches. Within a few minutes, he pinpointed where the nest had fallen from. John passed the nest up to him, and he wedged it as firmly as he could between several branches.

Rick climbed down, and I carefully climbed up, Robin Hood tucked safely in my palm. "Okay, little fellow. It's time to say goodbye. We're going to put you back in your home and hope your parents come right away to feed you and keep you nice and warm."

I realized that even if his parents returned, he might not survive. His siblings were already dead, and he looked close to death himself. He must have been cold, wet, and without food for many hours. I tucked him into the nest, praying that God would tend to one of His tiniest creatures. After I placed Robin Hood inside, I looked out across our yard. An adult robin studied us with great interest. Could it be one of Robin Hood's parents?

We removed the ladder and sat on our deck, far enough away that we wouldn't frighten Robin Hood's parents and prevent them from returning to the nest. I figured they must be confused and worried, wondering what happened to their home and family.

Minutes ticked slowly by. *Nothing.* What of the robin I'd seen watching us from the lawn? I'd been so sure that he or she would fly into the nest as soon as we'd gotten far enough away. Of course, I'd also been sure Ruth Zimmerman would survive cardiac arrest this morning, and now that appeared up in the air too.

After about 15 minutes, Rick stood up. "I've got stuff to do. Let me know how it goes." John followed him inside.

I nodded, my eyes remaining on the nest. On Robin Hood's fate. I felt that if I left, I would be giving up. A few more minutes passed, and then, the miraculous moment I'd been praying for took the form of two robins, in quick succession, flying to the nest. Robin Hood's parents had found him! My heart swelled with joy. Now, Robin Hood had a chance for survival. Just as Ruth still had a chance...

. . . .

The next day, I ran into Colleen at the grocery store.

"I heard Ruth coded four more times yesterday after we left the ED," she said. "They brought her back each time, but she coded again this morning." *Code* means to suffer a cardiac arrest. In other words, to be clinically dead.

I shuddered. "That's awful. How is she now?"

"She's in an induced coma," Colleen said. "It's not looking great. They think she may have cardiomyopathy but she's too unstable to fully assess. They had her on cooling blankets all day yesterday to lower her core temperature." Lowering a person's body temperature and inducing hypothermia slows the rate at which brain cells become damaged and die.

"If she pulls through, she'll need an internal defibrillator," I said. Her situation reminded me of cases in which young athletes drop dead from undiagnosed heart problems.

"That's for sure. I guess all we can do at this point is pray," Colleen said.

I nodded. "I was hoping to hear better news, but it sounds like she's still touch and go. Thanks for the update. I'll definitely keep her in my prayers."

After I returned home and unloaded the groceries, I stepped outside to check on Robin Hood. Perhaps I shouldn't have, but I couldn't resist. I pulled over the stepladder and peered into the nest. He was alive! Maybe it was my imagination, but he seemed like he had some feathers. He still appeared awfully fragile, and his tiny eyes were closed. I hoped saving him helped his parents alleviate some of their grief in losing their two other babies. At least it helped them to refocus their energy on saving him.

. . . .

The next day, I woke up early to the sound of my pager announcing a first aid call for a 68-year-old male with an ankle fracture. I slipped on a pair of sneakers, rinsed with mouthwash, and hustled to our building. When I entered the back of the ambulance, I found Colleen donning a pair of medical gloves.

"Any more news?" I asked as I fastened my seat belt.

"Ruth made it through the night. The doctor is starting to be a little more optimistic. They're going to try weaning her from sedation today to check her neuro status." *Neuro* is short for neurological. In other words, the doctor would check Ruth's cognitive function.

"It would be terrible to survive only to have brain damage," I said. "Hopefully, she'll be okay."

It was still hard for me to wrap my mind around the fact that a young woman could be healthy and swimming one minute and critically ill the next.

Colleen looked up from jotting down dispatch information on our call sheet. "My sister is friends with Ruth's cousin. Her cousin said Ruth was looking forward to going to her friend's wedding in ten days."

"I know it's unlikely, but it would be amazing if she could go."

Colleen crossed her fingers. "It sure would be."

Jessie called our rig on location. We found our patient, a tall thin fellow with thinning gray hair, sitting on his front-porch steps.

"I missed the last one," he said. "I hope it's just a sprain and not broken."

"You'll need an X-ray," Jessie said. We applied a cold pack and pillow splint, checked his vital signs, and transported him to Bakersville Hospital.

When I got home, I stepped out onto our deck. Robin Hood's parents were busy flying to and from the nest. From what I could tell, they were bringing him food. Just like Ruth, he was still hanging on.

. . . .

Each day, I watched Robin Hood's parents tending to his needs. I pictured him gaining weight and growing more feathers. Finally, about five days after Montana first found Robin Hood, I stepped outside and spotted him perched on a branch close to his nest. Now, he was a true fledgling rather than a nestling! My heart filled with joy at this miracle of life. Later that evening, Robin Hood flew out of the nest. I watched with glee as he cruised around our yard, testing his wings. How much his world expanded in a single day.

One week later

Ruth stared into a small handheld mirror. "Do I look okay?"

Carol smiled. "Are you kidding? You look fantastic. Of course, some of the credit goes to me, your wonderful hair stylist."

Ruth giggled. "Considering I'm in a hospital bed, you worked wonders with my hair."

"Now we have to slip you into your dress, then I'm going to scoot home to get ready myself. Just remember, I'll call you at six for the video call for Daisy's wedding. You're going to sit right in the church pew with me, friend."

"I'm truly sorry I can't go in person, but this is the next best thing. And I'm so happy I'll get to go home in a few days."

Carol hugged Ruth. "I'm so glad you're okay."

Ruth would need more testing in the future, but for now, she thanked God she was alive. Just like Robin Hood, she found her wings to fly.

He will cover you with his feathers,
and under his wings you will find refuge;
his faithfulness will be your shield and rampart.

PSALM 91:4

Chapter 18

Through the Ice!

The LORD is my strength and my shield;
my heart trusts in him, and he helps me.

PSALM 28:7

Two weeks of frigid days and nights created a thick layer of ice across Millwood Pond. It only took a few days for middle-schooler Gus Yawger to realize that if he cut across the pond, he could shave five minutes off his walk home from school. Not to mention, it was way more fun than walking along a boring sidewalk. The past few days trended warmer, making the trek across the pond even more pleasurable. No more icy wind slicing through him. Now, the sun's toasty rays warmed his face. Today, he looked at the pond with gleeful anticipation. Too bad Pine Cove didn't have more cold spells like this. He could get used to ice skating every day.

As he slipped and slid his way across the pond, Gus noticed a few puddles of water on the surface of the ice. He didn't give it much thought until he heard a loud cracking noise. The hair on the nape of his neck rose to full attention. He froze as he realized the ice beneath him began splitting.

What should I do? Trying to stifle the burgeoning fear inside him, he gradually lowered himself until he lay flat on his stomach. He thought he recalled hearing somewhere that it's better to lie down on ice if you're trying to rescue someone. He figured the same reasoning should apply to the person who needs rescuing. He tried to ignore the voice in his head that asked, *What if you fall through?* Slowly, Gus turned 180 degrees on his belly so that he was facing the shore. Ever so slowly, he began inching his way back toward land.

. . . .

Humming absentmindedly along with the radio, Lucy Parsons sprinkled chocolate chips into her brownie batter. She loved baking, and she wanted to surprise her four-year-old granddaughter with a special treat when she came to visit in a few hours. Lucy glanced out the window as she often did while working in her kitchen. She never tired of looking at the picturesque pond framed by breathtaking weeping willow trees. It reminded her of those old vacation postcards that say, "Greetings from…" on the front.

As she gazed out the window, a strange movement on the ice captured her attention. She blinked in disbelief and jerked the lacy window curtain aside. *Is that a child on the lake? With the past few warm days, that ice is probably paper thin. It'll never hold his weight!*

She grabbed her cordless telephone and dialed 911.

"Pine Cove Police. What is your emergency?" Dispatcher Jerome Franklin asked. Dispatcher Franklin, who had been working for the police department for about ten years, was an intelligent and well-respected member of the police department. He was known for being extremely dedicated to his job and the residents of Pine Cove.

"Hi, this is Mrs. Parsons. I'm looking out my kitchen window at Millwood Pond, and I see a child on the ice. I think it's Gus Yawger. I'm scared he's gonna fall through."

"Do you have eyes on him right now?" Franklin asked.

"Yes, he's lying on his stomach."

"Please don't take your eyes off the child. I'm sending patrolmen over immediately."

. . . .

Just as Gus came within about ten feet of the shore, the ice began cracking again. "Help!" he cried out before plunging through the ice into the frigid water, his entire body submerging below the surface. The frozen dungeon tried to claim him for its own.

Get your head out of the water. Gus struggled to bring his face to the surface. Everything seemed so dark. So frightening. Like all the light had been sucked out of the world, thrusting him into a universe of terror. Was the opening he created by falling through right over his head? Or had he drifted? What if he tried to push back upwards and there was ice over his head? Would he be able to somehow break through it?

Gus kicked as hard as he could and propelled his arms upwards toward what he prayed was the surface. The weight of his coat and pants dragged him downwards, but using all his might, he struggled toward the light. In that dark moment filled with uncertainty, his head and arms left the icy tomb and burst into the air. Taking gulps of air, he sucked oxygen into his starved lungs. He thrust his arms across the surface of the ice, but his torso and legs remained in the bitterly cold water. He tried kicking harder to pull the rest of himself up out of the water and onto the ice. However, the slippery surface refused to cooperate with his plan. No matter how hard he kicked, he didn't get any closer to freeing himself.

. . . .

"Of course, I'll keep my eyes on him," Lucy stammered as she spoke to Dispatcher Franklin. "Right now, he's lying on his stomach. It looks like he's trying to get back to the shore. Oh, no! He fell through!"

Dropping the phone, she rushed outdoors toward the pond, her apron flapping in the breeze. Pushing 75 years old, Lucy's days of jogging had long ago retreated to her past. Now, filled with a sense of desperate purpose, she willed her legs to keep moving forward, all the while keeping her eyes glued on the spot where Gus fell through.

"Gus, it's me, Mrs. Parsons. I need you to hang in there!"

She had no idea if he could even hear her. As she yelled, she could hear police sirens in the distance. *Thank God, help is on the way!*

Just then, Lucy's neighbor, Ned Hawkins, raced toward her.

Although approaching middle age, he managed to remain fit with a rigorous exercise regimen. "I heard all the yelling. What's going on?"

"Gus fell through the ice! I called 911, and the police are on the way." As Lucy spoke, Gus's head broke through the water's surface. "Gus, we're going to help you!"

Gus gasped for air. "Please get me out of here!"

Ned grabbed a large oak branch that lay close by. "Gus, I don't think the water is deep right here. I think you might be able to put your feet on the bottom."

Gus stopped kicking and did as Ned suggested. "You're right. I can touch." Exhausted from the stress, strain, and frigid temperatures, he felt relief that he could stop kicking. But his legs were turning numb.

Ned lay on his stomach on the ground and slid the branch out as far as he could. "Grab hold of it!"

Although his arms felt like they had morphed into concrete, Gus reached forward and strained with all his might until he could reach the very tip of the branch with his right hand.

"You've almost got it, buddy. Now, get a better grip," Ned said.

Gus lunged further, grasping the end of the branch more firmly in his small hand.

"Squeeze tight now," Ned commanded urgently. "Grab on with your other hand too, and then on the count of three, push on the bottom as hard as you can. I'm going to pull you in. You can do this."

"Okay," Gus whispered, reaching for the branch with his left hand as well. He wrapped his numb fingers around the branch as tightly as possible.

"One, two, three!" Ned shouted, hoping Gus had enough strength and energy to hang on.

. . . .

I'd taken a half day from work so I could catch up on errands and housecleaning. Fortunately, I had my pager turned to vibrate mode as I was vacuuming. I quickly switched off the vacuum so I could hear the dispatcher's message.

Although I've been trained in ice rescue, I've never been on a first aid call for a person who's fallen through the ice. Heart racing, I hopped into my car and rushed to the first aid building. As I arrived, I saw Mason Chapman jogging across the street toward the squad headquarters. Alec Waters, currently home on break from veterinary school, stood in front of the building. I was glad to see him, for he's knowledgeable and highly skilled in EMS.

"We'll need to hook the boat up for this one," he said. "I'll bring the ambulance out onto the apron, and you guys can pull the boat up behind it."

Mason grabbed the left side of the boat, while I took hold of the right. We rolled the boat in line with the rear of the rig and hitched the boat trailer to the ambulance. Although it took only a minute or two, it seemed like an eternity as I thought about the child submerged in frigid water. *Will we get there in time to rescue him?*

Alec jumped into the driver's seat and grabbed the mic. "We're in service to Millwood Pond." He flipped on the emergency lights and pulled out onto the roadway.

"Received. Use the southern access. Bystanders are attempting to get the juvenile out of the water. Patrols are arriving on scene now," Dispatcher Franklin updated us.

In the back of the rig, I cranked the heat so it would be toasty warm for our victim. Alec expertly weaved the ambulance through traffic until he pulled up close to Millwood Pond. A man with a long branch, assisted by several police officers and firefighters, was pulling a boy across the ice to safety. When he neared the edge of the pond, they hoisted him up and placed him safely onto the nearby ground. Carrying a pile of blankets, I hurried toward our patient. His small frame shivered violently, and his lips had a bluish hue.

"Gus took a spill through the ice, but he's feeling okay," Officer

Endicott said, supporting the child around his shoulders. "His mom's on the way here."

"Hi, Gus. Let's get you out of this cold and into the warm ambulance," Mason said. He wrapped one of the blankets around Gus, scooped him into his arms, and carried him across the snow into our nearby rig.

Gus's teeth chattered loudly.

"We're going to warm you up," I said.

Alec, Mason, and I stripped off Gus's wet clothing and dried him off with towels. Then we wrapped him in a mylar emergency blanket designed to reflect radiated body heat and help prevent hypothermia. We placed multiple blankets on top, nestling him in a warm cocoon. Gradually, the shivering diminished.

Now with danger over, Gus grew somber. "I was taking a shortcut home. My mom's gonna kill me."

Almost on cue, an ashen-faced woman swung open the rear ambulance door. Officer Endicott assisted her up the large step into the rig. She bent over the stretcher and hugged Gus tightly.

"Gus, are you okay?"

Gus nodded. "I'm fine. I'm really sorry."

"How many times have I told you not to…"

Gus didn't give her a chance to finish her sentence, for he knew what she was going to say. We could all fill in the blank. *How many times have I told you not to walk across the ice?*

"I know. A lot, I guess," Gus replied. Between the heat blasting and the effective hypothermia blanket, Gus's color gradually returned to normal. "I feel much better already, Mom."

"Would you like us to take Gus to the hospital to get checked out?" Mason asked.

"No thanks. I'm good," Gus said before his mother could reply. "I'm all better. I promise."

Mrs. Yawger placed her hand on his forehead, gauging his temperature. "Well, if you're sure you're okay, I can take you straight to the pediatrician instead of the hospital."

"Okay, but maybe we should go home and have a few chocolate-chip cookies first," Gus said, a smile lighting his face. Thanks to the resiliency of youth, the terror of moments ago faded into the past.

Mrs. Yawger smiled. "Oh, you and your cookies."

As mother and son hugged, I reflected on today's events. *What a blessing that his neighbor looked out her window at exactly the right moment! How fortunate that a strong, able-bodied neighbor heard the cries for help and came right away.* I felt like it was through God's grace that these two amazing neighbors and a team of first responders came together to rescue a precious child. *A miraculous save choreographed and orchestrated by our heavenly Father.*

Chapter 19

The Premonition

So then, just as you received Christ Jesus as Lord,
continue to live your lives in him, rooted and built
up in him, strengthened in the faith as you were
taught, and overflowing with thankfulness.

COLOSSIANS 2:6-7

I settled back into my seat next to my husband, Rick, as I waited for the Saturday evening church service to begin. It'd been a long, busy day, and I looked forward to having some quiet time to reflect. I studied the familiar ornate stained-glass windows, enjoying how the late afternoon sun illuminated them. Soon, the service began with an entrance song and opening prayers.

After a brief time, I began to get an odd feeling that we would have a first aid call in the back of the church, behind where I was sitting. I wondered how I would know if there was a call, since I don't bring my pager into church. What if someone needed help, but I didn't realize it?

I brushed the odd feeling aside and tried to concentrate on our minister's message. About ten minutes later, I felt a firm tap on my left shoulder. One of the church ushers stood next to me. "We need your help," he whispered.

I jumped up and followed him to the rear of the church, about fifteen pews from where I'd been sitting. The usher pointed to an older gentleman with thick white hair who sat slumped forward in his seat.

"Call 911," I said to the usher, then slipped into the seat next to our patient. An older woman sat on the other side of him. I guessed she must be his wife.

"Hi, I'm with the first aid squad," I said. I kept my voice very soft as the service was still going on.

Near-palpable waves of fear and anxiety emanated from the woman. "I'm Candace. Thank God you're here. Harold isn't responding at all."

I lifted his head to open his airway and noted the stark whiteness of his face. His face glistened with perspiration, and his shirt was soaked with sweat.

"Harold, can you hear me?"

Harold stared vacantly ahead, oblivious to my presence. I slid my fingers onto his wrist. His pulse was 96, weak but regular. His respirations were about 20 and shallow.

"Can you tell me how he's been today?" I asked.

Candace placed her hand on Harold's right thigh. "We're from Pennsylvania. We came here early this morning to spend the weekend. He seemed fine all day. He didn't complain about anything. But about ten minutes ago, I started to notice that something seemed off. He started leaning forward in this chair. I kept trying to get his attention, but he didn't respond. That's when I flagged the usher for help."

"Does he have any cardiac history, like problems with his heart? Did he drink any fluids today?"

"He doesn't have any medical problems. Harold's always been healthy. But now that you mention it, he hasn't drunk much water today. He was afraid if he had too much, he'd have to go to the bathroom."

I'd become so focused on Harold that I didn't notice the service had stopped. I glanced up and realized our minister stood over us, saying prayers of healing. Harold gradually began responding.

"What happened?" he asked.

"You nearly passed out," I said. "An ambulance is on the way to take you to the hospital to get checked out."

Just then, Officer Brad Sims arrived. He handed me a blood-pressure cuff and a pulse oximeter. Harold's blood pressure was low (94/60), but his oxygen saturation level remained normal at 98 percent.

"I'm starting to feel a little better," Harold said.

First aid squad members Jessie Barnes and Colin Branigan entered with a stair chair and first aid bag. I helped Harold shift onto the chair, which is small enough to fit into the elevator in the back of the church. When we got outside, we moved him onto our stretcher.

Colin's pager began beeping. "It sounds like we're getting another call," he said.

DISPATCHER: "Request for first aid at 501 Hanover Road for a female with difficulty breathing."

I slipped a pillow behind Harold's head. "Another crew will have to handle that one. We already have our hands full."

Candace appeared close to tears. She touched Harold's hand. "I'm so upset, I'm not sure I can drive. And I don't know my way around here."

Jessie patted her arm. "I'll drive your car for you."

A look of profound relief washed over Candace's face. "You would do that?"

"Of course," Jessie replied. "That way, you'll have your car with you when he gets released."

Colin got behind the steering wheel of the ambulance, and Jessie walked away with Candace. I was glad Rick had my car keys because he'd need them to get home. I climbed into the back of the ambulance to continue caring for Harold. His condition improved steadily on the way to the hospital. I hoped he was simply dehydrated, and some IV fluids would make him as good as new and they could enjoy the rest of their weekend getaway.

Usually, we don't hear how our patients do. Several weeks later, I was pleasantly surprised at our business meeting when our secretary began reading a letter aloud.

Dear Pine Cove First Aid Squad,

I would like to thank you for saving my husband's life at church a few weeks ago. I was so scared! Imagine my surprise when one of your members, Andrea, jumped up to help. God sent us help when we needed it most. A special thank you to Jessie for driving me to the hospital. I was much too upset and frazzled to drive myself. Please accept this donation as a token of our appreciation.

Sincerely,
Candace and Harold

I have no idea why I had a premonition that there would be a first aid call behind me that day at church. I imagine it was God's hand at work, making sure people were available to help His followers when they asked for aid.

Chapter 20

Rescuing One of God's Children

But you, LORD, do not be far from me.
You are my strength; come quickly to help me.

PSALM 22:19

imon Oliver let out a whoop of delight as he sprinted through Pine Cove Park alongside his friends Corey and Ben. The smell of honeysuckle and the promise of warm summer days clung to the air. "Race you to the lake!" he hollered.

"You're on!" Corey said, the pent-up energy from a long school day erupting like lava from an overdue volcano.

The friends dashed across a grassy field, past a basketball court, and toward Weeping Willow Lake.

"Just try to catch up with me," Simon shouted gleefully.

Ben laughed. "Yeah right. I'm going to leave you in the dust."

Ben and Corey ran on their school's track team and each accrued numerous blue ribbons over the course of the season. Soon, they pulled ahead of Simon.

As Simon saw his friends pass by, bright colors began exploding all around him. He tried to call his friends to stop, but no words came out. His legs began to wobble, and an odd sensation coursed through his body. He sank to his knees before awkwardly crashing onto his left side.

Unaware that Simon had fallen, Corey and Ben raced ahead. Corey reached the lake's shore first, followed closely by Ben. Both paused to catch their breath.

Ben savored the cool breeze that blew across the lake. "I wish I had some nice cold water."

"You can drink some lake water," Corey said as the two began a friendly scuffle, rolling on the ground near the water's edge.

Suddenly, Corey sat bolt upright. "Hey, where's Simon? He should be here by now." The two boys jumped to their feet and looked back toward the field they'd just run across.

Ben frowned. "I don't see him." Puzzled, the two boys began to retrace their steps.

Corey pointed ahead. "Hey, I think he's lying down in the grass. He must have gotten tired."

"Or he's goofing on us," Ben said. "It wouldn't be the first time."

They jogged over to where Simon lay.

"Are you okay?" Ben asked. He noticed Simon had a faraway look in his eyes. "I think something's wrong. I don't think he's faking."

Corey knelt next to Simon and shook his shoulder. "Don't mess around, dude. If you're kidding, it's not funny."

Ben knelt on Simon's other side, the freshly cut grass sticking to his bare knees. "Doesn't Simon have epilepsy?"

"Epi-what?" Corey asked.

"Epilepsy," Ben said. "You know, seizures. I wonder if he's going to have a seizure or if he already had one while we were down by the lake. I have a cousin with epilepsy."

Simon's arms and legs began shaking uncontrollably. Bubbles foamed from the corner of his mouth.

Corey rocked back onto his heels. "What's happening? What should we do?"

Ben leaned forward. "He's having a seizure. We need to make sure he can breathe, and we need to get help right away. He's clenching his jaw, and I don't think he's getting enough air."

Just then, Simon's head rolled back, but his jaw remained firmly shut.

"I think you're right," Corey said. "His face is turning blue."

"You're going to be okay, Simon," Ben said with more confidence than he felt. He cast a worried look toward Corey.

Corey pointed to a white Colonial across the street from the park. "I'm going to run over there and ask for help. If no one's home, I'll keep ringing doorbells until I find someone."

Ben nodded. "Tell them to call 911 and that Simon is having a seizure."

Corey jumped to his feet and rushed away.

Ben turned back toward Simon. "I know you don't mean to, but you're really scaring me. Please be okay." Ben knew when his cousin had a seizure, he would be confused and "out of it" for a little while. But Simon's seizure didn't seem to be ending. Instead, his entire body continued to shake and thrash with convulsions.

. . . .

DISPATCHER: "Request for first aid on the north side of Weeping Willow Park for a twelve-year-old boy actively seizing."

I met Colleen Harper at the first aid building.

"There's already one EMT at the scene, so we can roll," she said. I hopped into the front passenger seat, and we drove a short distance to Weeping Willow Park.

Squad member Mason Chapman met us at the ambulance. "I was literally biking by when the call went out. We're going to need oxygen, the first aid kit, and the stretcher. He's definitely going to need transport. Officer Endicott is with him now."

We rolled the stretcher, piled with our rescue equipment, across the grassy field. As we got closer, I spotted a young boy with sandy blond hair lying on his side in the grass. From a glance, I could see he was still convulsing. Another young boy, who looked to be about the same age, stood close by.

"Is this your friend?" Colleen asked gently. "Can you tell us what happened?"

Ben nodded. "Simon, Corey, and I were having a race. When Corey and I got to the lake, we realized that Simon wasn't with us anymore. We went back to look for him, and when we found him, he had a weird look on his face. Then he started shaking all over, like he's doing now. Corey ran to get help, and I stayed here with Simon."

Just then, Corey returned and huddled next to Ben. "Is he going to be okay?" Corey asked.

Mason patted Corey's shoulder. "We're going to take good care of Simon and take him to the hospital. You two did a fantastic job." He placed Simon on high-flow oxygen using a non-rebreather mask.

I knelt next to Simon and checked his pulse. "It's 88, strong and regular," I said to Colleen, who was jotting down notes. "I can't get a blood pressure or pulse ox. He's moving too much."

"Have we been able to contact Simon's parents?" Colleen asked.

"Ben was able to give us Simon's phone number and address. Since the dispatcher couldn't get ahold of Simon's parents by phone, he sent an officer to the house. Once he gains contact with them, he'll tell them to meet you at the hospital," Officer Endicott said.

I spotted a little blood in the corner of Simon's mouth. I figured he probably bit his tongue while seizing. "What's the ETA on the medics?"

"About three minutes," Officer Endicott replied.

"Okay. Let's get him on the stretcher and into the rig so we'll be ready to go when the medics get here," Colleen said.

I held Simon's head and protected his airway while we carefully lifted him onto the stretcher. For a brief minute, his limbs were quiet, but then his small body began to clench and thrash again.

After Officer Endicott and Mason lifted the stretcher into our ambulance, Colleen switched the portable oxygen to the large onboard unit. I used a small catheter to suction away the saliva that bubbled out of Simon's nose and mouth.

Kennisha Smythe and Arthur Williamson, paramedics who provide advanced life support, stepped into the rig.

"How long has he been seizing?" Arthur asked as he placed his gear on the ambulance bench.

"At this point, it's probably going on 12 minutes," Mason said. "He briefly stopped a few times, but then it started right back up again."

Arthur checked Simon's arm to establish IV access. "It sounds like he's in status epilepticus. We need to expedite."

Status epilepticus means a seizure lasting five minutes or more with continuous clinical or electrographic seizure activity or recurrent seizures without recovery in between them. It's considered an extremely dangerous medical emergency.

"I'll drive your ambulance," Mason said.

"Great," Kennisha said, tossing him the keys. "Let's go."

Colleen returned to the driver's seat and picked up the mic. "We're going to Bakersville Hospital," she told dispatch.

As we headed toward the emergency department, Simon's limbs gradually quieted, but he remained unresponsive. He looked small and vulnerable as he lay on our stretcher. My heart went out to him and his parents.

"I just got word from the police department," Colleen called back to us from the driver's seat. "They found Simon's parents, and they're going to meet us at the hospital."

I wasn't sure if Simon could hear me, but I held his hand and relayed Colleen's message. I hoped the words would bring him some measure of comfort.

Arthur took advantage of Simon's stillness to secure the intravenous line in his left arm. No sooner had he finished, Simon began seizing again.

"Kennisha, when you call the ED, ask if the pediatric intensivist can meet us there," I said. "He's definitely going to be admitted to the PICU." As a physical therapist, I sometimes work with patients in the pediatric intensive care unit (PICU). I prayed Simon would recover quickly and be able to participate in rehab with me soon.

"Got it. At the rate he's going, he may need to be intubated and sedated when we get there," Kennisha replied.

Arthur nodded. "This is one sick little boy."

As we backed into a parking spot in the ED's parking garage, I spotted an anxious looking couple, who appeared to be in their mid-forties, standing near the entrance. I realized they must be Simon's parents.

As we lifted the stretcher out of the ambulance, Mrs. Oliver caught sight of Simon and rushed over to us. Her face turned stark white. "What happened to my baby?" Mr. Oliver threw his arm around her shoulders to support her. I got the sense that if he let go, she would collapse onto the asphalt.

"How's our son?" Mr. Oliver asked. "We got here as fast as we could."

"He's been seizing on and off for a half hour," Arthur said. "The pediatric team will be meeting us in the emergency room. Has he ever had an episode like this before?"

Mr. Oliver shook his head. "He's had three seizures in the past five years, but none of them lasted for more than a few minutes."

We rolled Simon into the pediatric area, setting off a flurry of activity. After we transferred Simon to the hospital's stretcher, I turned slowly away and said a silent prayer that he would recover quickly and completely.

. . . .

Several days passed, and I received physician's orders to provide physical therapy to a child in the PICU. When I arrived, I realized the child I would be evaluating happened to be in the room directly next to Simon's. I peeked in and my heart clenched. Simon was covered in wires and tubes. The doctors had intubated him, so now a tube in his airway was connected to a ventilator, breathing for him. His eyes were closed, and he appeared to be unresponsive. The next day, I checked again. He didn't look any better. I tried to stifle my discouragement and trust in God's plan.

Days passed. Early the next week, I received physical therapy orders for Simon himself. I tried to contain my excitement. Just because I received orders didn't necessarily mean he was doing better. Sometimes, even though a patient is unresponsive, we'll receive orders to perform passive range-of-motion exercises. That way, the person's joints won't get too stiff during the period of time they aren't moving them on their own. Other times, if a patient is more alert, we'll receive PT orders to get him or her out of bed to a chair.

When I entered Simon's room, I found him sitting in a high-back chair with a small footstool under his feet. He smiled when he spotted me.

"Hi. Are you the PT? Can we go for a walk? My nurse said you were coming, and we could try walking in the hall together."

My spirits lifted. Simon's eyes shone bright and clear, in marked contrast to a week ago. Previously pale cheeks now boasted a healthy pink color.

"Of course," I said, delighted to see such a profound change for the better in his medical condition. "Nothing would make me happier!"

My heart sang as we strolled down the hallway and back. It would just be a matter of time before Simon could once again run in the park with his friends. I marveled how fortunate he was to be with two smart, caring friends when he began seizing, rather than alone somewhere. In addition, someone answered the door of the first house Corey went to for help, allowing EMS to be activated as quickly as possible. Not to mention when we were dispatched, one of our squad members just happened to be cycling past.

Once again, God put the cogs in motion to orchestrate a rescue of one of His children.

Chapter 21

The Answered Prayers

Mightier than the thunder of the great waters,
mightier than the breakers of the sea—
the LORD on high is mighty.

PSALM 93:4

Even though I'm grown up now, Labor Day weekend creates a yearning for summer to continue. Memories of childhood surface, making me feel like I'm not ready to go back to school yet. A wave of bittersweet nostalgia envelopes me, pulling me back to the days of leisurely swimming in our town's large pool and in the Atlantic. It didn't matter if the chilly water grew goosebumps across my arms and legs. Those days brought pure, unmitigated joy to life.

Now, I tried to shake loose the dismal feeling that Labor Day brings. Soon, the children of Pine Cove would be trading beach towels for book bags. Goggles for pens. Snorkels for pencils. You get the idea. My musings ended abruptly when my pager went off.

> **DISPATCHER:** *"Request for first aid and fire department for a smell of gas. Location being determined by patrols."*

I figured a family was trying to squeeze out the last bit of summer with an afternoon barbeque. I certainly couldn't blame them. I jumped in my car and headed for the first aid building, where I met up with Jessie Barnes, Helen McGuire, and Archie Harris.

"Hop in, and I'll pull out onto the apron. We're still waiting for an exact location," Jessie said.

I slipped into the back and pulled a pair of gloves from the wall dispenser. I figured I probably wouldn't need them for this call, so I held them in my lap. Sometimes, calls for the smell of gas end of up being unfounded. For example, the smell could be due to a neighbor's barbeque or a backyard firepit. I buckled my seat belt in anticipation of our response.

. . . .

As the mother of a three-year-old and a fourteen-month-old, Cynthia Downs appreciated the warm September sun's rays, but she was too busy to fully enjoy them. Her children, which were her world, kept her super busy. Her husband, Jim, wanted to do something special to celebrate the last days of summer, so they rented a shore home, a welcome change from their apartment in the city. Cynthia enjoyed the chance to let her children enjoy the nearby beach and the in-ground pool in the backyard of their rental home. The ultra-blue water sparkled magically, inviting relief from the warm sun.

Jim's cell phone began ringing. He glanced at the caller information. "Sorry, I have to take this. It's work," he apologized, rising to his feet from a lounge chair. He spoke in hushed tones for a few minutes before heading inside into the quiet of the home.

Baby Eva, an active fourteen-month-old, sat in the shade of a sun umbrella. Bright and determined, she focused on placing colorful blocks into a shape sorter. Her small brows furrowed as she concentrated on fitting the blue cylinder through the circular shape on the top of the block cannister.

Cynthia's son, Todd, a robust and energetic three-year-old, squealed with delight. "Mom, watch this!" He pushed his small blue-and-white tugboat through the water at the shallow end of the pool. "Did you see? Did you see?"

"Yes, look at that little boat go. You make a good ship captain," Cynthia replied.

She turned to check on Baby Eva, who shortly ago sat about 15 feet from the pool's edge. The cannister of blocks lay on its side, with several of the blocks scattered about. Frantically, Cynthia's eyes scanned the large backyard. *No sign of Eva. Where could she be?* She tried to quell the rising panic within. She whipped her head around, scarcely believing her eyes. Eva, her sweet, angelic baby, lay facedown in the deep end of the pool, floating near the surface.

Cynthia jumped into the pool, taking several short crawl strokes with her head out of the water so she could keep her eyes on Eva. When she reached her, she flipped her over onto her back. Eva's eyes were closed, her face blue, her body limp. Cynthia felt as if she had been suddenly pulled from real life and dumped into some kind of horror movie.

Cynthia pulled Eva close and performed several side strokes until she could reach the edge of the pool. She hoisted herself and Eva out, quickly rising to her feet. *What should I do?* Eva's head hung back, foam bubbling from the corners of her mouth.

Cynthia thought back to several years ago when she'd been certified in CPR. She recalled giving back blows to an infant, but that was for a choking victim. Was drowning the same as choking? She began giving sharp back blows between Eva's shoulder blades while simultaneously screaming for help.

. . . .

DISPATCHER: "Priority reassignment for first aid. Respond to 401 Bergen Street for an unconscious baby."

Jessie promptly picked up the ambulance's mic. "We're in service with a two-minute ETA." He flipped on the overhead lights and pulled off the building's apron, using his siren to move traffic out of our way.

Often, our calls for infants involve febrile seizures or falls. So far with this call, there wasn't a whole lot of information. What had caused the baby's unconsciousness? I pulled the foldable child seat and pediatric kit out of the overhead cabinet before fastening my seat belt. The pedi kit has pint-sized equipment, such as extra small blood-pressure cuffs, oxygen masks, nasal cannulas, and bag valve masks. I began unrolling the child seat so it would be ready to strap to the stretcher if needed.

> **DISPATCHER:** "Update: the baby is out of the pool. Be advised you have one member at the scene."

Out of the pool? I hadn't realized the infant was in a pool! Suddenly, the alarming nature of this call grew exponentially. If an infant was found unconscious in a pool, how long had they been submerged? Was the baby breathing? Had the baby swallowed water? Did some pool water go into the lungs?

Drowning is the number one cause of death for children under the age of four. There are over 4,000 unintentional fatal drownings each year in the United States. That's a chilling 11 deaths per day. Even if a child is rescued, he or she may suffer permanent brain damage and disability. My heart hammered in my chest. I said a quick, silent prayer that the baby would be okay.

Archie pulled the suction unit out of a cabinet on his left. "It sounds like we may have a near-drowning."

"How awful," Helen said. "I wonder how long the baby was under." She began preparing the defibrillator and several towels in case we needed them. To shock a person with an AED, the chest must be dry. Joules of energy and water don't mix.

"I bet Ted O'Malley is the one who's on the scene," I said. Ted lived a few blocks from Bergen Street.

Jessie jockeyed through the intersections, blaring his siren to pass safely through side streets until we arrived at the scene. "We're on location," he notified dispatch, throwing the rig into park. "You guys go ahead, and I'll finish setting up the infant seat."

A concerned elderly neighbor leaning heavily on an aluminum cane met us at the curb. She pointed toward the rear of a gray clapboard home. "Hurry, they're in the back."

"Thank you," I murmured.

Helen, Archie, and I rushed past her down a red paver driveway and through a tall white privacy gate into a spacious backyard with a large crystal-blue pool. My guess about the first aid member on the scene was correct. Ted O'Malley stood next to a distraught young woman who held a limp baby girl in her arms.

Ted turned toward us. "This is Eva Downs. She's conscious and breathing now. I checked her lung sounds, and I hear some congestion." He held a pediatric oxygen mask in front of her tiny face, allowing oxygen-rich air to blow by her face. "Let's get her in the ambulance. We can check her vital signs there."

I could hear Eva cough weakly. I figured her body was trying to expel any residual pool water from her lungs. In an acute near drowning, laryngospasm occurs after ingesting a small amount of water. This causes water to be ingested into the stomach. However, when the laryngospasm relaxes due to hypoxia (lack of oxygen), large amounts of water can be aspirated into (enter into) the lungs.

Helen placed a hand on the mother's shoulder. "Follow me. We're going to lead you to the ambulance. Would you like me to carry Eva?"

Mrs. Downs shook her head. "No, I'll do it."

I think after such a close brush with death, she didn't want to let her daughter go. And although she was alive, she was far from out of the woods.

"Do you have someone to watch your son?" Helen asked.

"Yes, my husband has him now. He's going to follow us by car to the hospital," Mrs. Downs replied. Once we entered the ambulance, Eva began coughing more. I rechecked her lung sounds. "I can hear abnormal sounds during exhalation. Hopefully, her coughing will bring the rest of the water out." Next, I placed a tiny pulse oximeter on Eva's finger. "Her pulse ox is 93 percent." Instead of blow-by oxygen, I secured the strap around her head to give her a higher concentration of oxygen.

I wrapped the infant cuff around Eva's right upper arm. "Her blood pressure is 108 over 58 and her pulse is 137." I noticed her pale cheeks began to grow pinker. *A good sign.*

"The medics are pulling up now," Helen said.

We took Eva from Cynthia's arms and strapped her into the infant child seat, which Jessie had already secured to our stretcher. Now, the medics would be able to perform their assessment without wasting valuable time at the scene. I knew with a call like this, rapid transport to the hospital is critical. Next, Helen helped Cynthia secure her own seat belt. If possible, our squad allows one parent to ride in the back of the ambulance with us.

Paramedics Rose Anderson and William Moore climbed aboard the rig and began their assessment. "Now that Eva's had a few minutes of oxygen, let's see what the pulse ox reading is on room air." She slid the mask off. "It's 97 percent now. That's good. We can keep the oxygen off." *Another good sign.*

As Eva continued to improve on the way to the hospital, some of Cynthia's near-palpable anxiety eased. "We're renting the home for a few weeks. I asked for one without a pool, but this was the only one available."

After careful testing, the emergency department staff determined that Eva had no more water in her lungs. She was kept overnight for observation but made a full recovery. *A heaven-sent miracle!* Now, Eva and her family embraced the promise of tomorrow, a future life in Christ brimming with hope and wonder. A life with God at their side.

. . . .

A few weeks later, as an unusually strong late September sun cast its rays upon beach sunbathers, I was reminded of Baby Eva. Since Labor Day slipped past several weeks ago, lifeguards no longer guarded the surf. Numerous beachgoers decided the allure of the ocean justified the risk.

Waves pounded along the shoreline, white frothy foam swirling along the water's edge. Two tropical storms, too far out to sea to affect the weather, created towering waves and dangerous rip currents. A rip current is a powerful, fast-moving surface current that carries water from the shore, returning the water carried in by waves. Rip currents can reach up to 150 feet wide, but more commonly they're less than 30 feet across. They can move at speeds up to five miles per hour, which is faster than most people can swim. On this day, most people were enjoying the waves and not worrying about potential hazards.

Dora Creighton stretched in her beach chair, digging her toes into the sand. She raised her lashes and sneaked a peek sideways at her companion. She'd been dating Ed Jaxson for the past two months. They'd both parted ways with their spouses about a year ago. Devastated after the divorce, Dora now felt ready to enter the dating world again. She enjoyed taking day trips and dining out with Ed. Nothing too serious yet. Dora was content to keep it that way for now. She liked Ed but didn't want to rush into a serious relationship.

"It's getting hot. Why don't we take a dip?" she suggested.

"Sure," Ed agreed. He rose to his feet and offered Dora his hand. "It looks rough. Let's stay close to the shore."

Dora nodded. She wasn't a strong swimmer, but the idea of cooling off tempted her. She drifted into the waves. "I can't believe how warm it is." Playfully, she splashed some water at Ed.

As they stepped further into the waves, a young woman passed them coming out. "Be careful. It's rough," she warned.

"We will. Thanks," Ed replied. He slipped his hand into Dora's, gently pulling her closer to his side. The sun beat on their shoulders, enticing them further into the refreshing water.

The pair chatted about everything from their favorite movies to past jobs to where they went to college. Dora didn't intend to go into the ocean past her knees, but suddenly a series of large waves thundered upon them, ripping her hand from Ed's. Water swirled around her chest. She pinched her nose and went under the first wave, then again for the second. Ditto for the third. As she held her breath and ducked under a fourth wave, it caught her in its angry grip, twirling her like a load of laundry in the spin cycle and pounding her into the ocean floor.

Momentarily disoriented, Dora struggled to regain her footing. As her head bobbed to the surface, she realized with dismay she could no longer touch the ocean floor. She began treading water, but her arms and legs quickly grew fatigued. She spotted Ed closer to the shoreline. Though the waves had pulled her far out, he managed somehow to stay closer to the beach.

Dora tried to lift her arms to signal for help, but heavy anchors pulled them downwards. Focused on the shoreline, she didn't see the giant wave approaching. It smashed across her, throwing her face forward into the salty water. She swallowed a bunch as she rolled onto her back, coughing and gagging. *Keep kicking. Keep treading.*

But even as she told herself to keep fighting, weariness overtook her. Her arms and legs ached, screaming for rest. She sensed the world around her growing darker. In that moment, she feared she would surely die. Death wound its tentacles around her, marking her as its next victim. A long tunnel stretched before her, sucking her within. Just before losing consciousness, she made a desperate plea to God for help.

. . . .

Ed dragged himself from the water, staggering onto the beach. *Where's Dora?* Frantically, his eyes scanned the water. His heart raced, pounding in his chest so hard that he grew lightheaded. Then, at last, he caught a glimpse of Dora's face just as it sank below the sea's surface.

"Help!" he cried out. Exhausted, he sank to his knees. He wasn't much of a swimmer. There was no way he could help her.

Numerous bystanders rushed toward him. "My girlfriend is drowning," he said, pointing in the direction he had last seen Dora.

"I'll call 911," a middle-aged woman said as five brave men and women swam out into the rough surf.

Ed rose to his feet and waded into the water up to his knees. Fervently, he prayed they'd find Dora. *Alive.* Long seconds stretched into miserable minutes. He watched as the would-be rescuers motioned to each other, searching the area. Could they find her? Would it be too late if they did?

Then, unmistakably, over the thundering surf, he heard a voice cry out, "I've got her!" One of the rescuers wrapped his arm around Dora's chest, holding her limp head above the water's surface. He performed the sidestroke as he towed her closer to the shoreline. When they reached shallow water, many strong arms of concerned bystanders pulled Dora further up the beach onto dry sand.

A surfer knelt next to Dora and placed his fingers alongside her neck. "She doesn't have a pulse. I'm starting CPR." He opened Dora's airway and then placed clasped hands over the center of her sternum and performed vigorous chest compressions. After about 15 compressions, Dora began to wretch. He turned her to her side, and she began vomiting torrents of ocean water. After a few moments, her eyes popped open as she began gasping for air.

"I've got a radial pulse of 80. It's strong and regular," the surfer said. "Is an ambulance on the way?"

. . . .

My family and I made our way through the streets of Pine Cove toward Marina Beach, where we planned to have dinner with my sister Marie. As Rick drove our car, my first aid pager activated.

DISPATCHER: "Request for the first aid squad at the Hudson Avenue Beach for an unconscious person, now conscious. Possible heat exhaustion."

We were a few miles from the first aid building, so I knew I wouldn't catch the ambulance. I asked Rick if we could stop at the scene on the way to my sister's house. Volunteer EMT Helen McGuire called in service and began driving toward the scene of the call. Almost immediately, my pager went off again.

DISPATCHER: "Request for the first aid squad at the Wesley Avenue Beach for a drowning. Expedite. CPR in progress."

"That's two different beach calls in as many minutes. Which one do you want to go to?" Rick asked.

I began donning a pair of medical gloves, which I'd pulled out of a cupholder in my car door. Before I could answer Rick, Jessie Barnes keyed up the mic on a second ambulance. "We'll be in service to Wesley Avenue with a short crew. All available members, please go directly to the scene."

Rick headed toward Wesley Avenue beach. The surf had been churning the past few days due to a tropical storm out at sea. In fact, someone had drowned in a nearby town just yesterday. Rick began jockeying along side streets as he made his way toward the first aid call. He pulled up in the yellow no-parking zone alongside the dunes at the beach entrance.

"You go ahead to Marie's. I'll catch up with you later," I said, then rushed along the dune-lined path to the boardwalk. A large crowd had already gathered, watching the attempted rescue unfold. I slipped through the crowd and rushed down the stairs to the sand, heading toward a group of people close to the shoreline. I figured I'd find our victim in the middle of them. As I grew closer, I met Officer Vinnie McGovern.

"Bystanders pulled her out of the water," he said. "She was initially unconscious, and they said they did CPR for a minute. She's conscious now. Sandy Springs still had some lifeguards on duty this weekend. They got the call and came over on their ATV. They're putting her on a backboard now. She's got a history of asthma, and she swallowed a lot of water."

"Thanks for the update," I said, studying the scene. Numerous lifeguards in navy blue bathing suits knelt around the victim. Jessie crouched near the woman's head, protecting her airway. Member Kerry Branson knelt nearby, pulling an oxygen tank from our first aid bag.

Officer McGovern pointed to a tall man wearing a black-and-white striped bathing suit and white shirt. "That's her boyfriend. You can get more information from him."

As I drew closer, I could see the lifeguards were almost done strapping a middle-aged woman to a spinal immobilization board. The board would be used to carry her off the beach. Once she could be safely placed on our stretcher, we could slide the board out from under her. I picked up our notepad from the top of our rescue bag and introduced myself to the woman's boyfriend.

"Can I ask you some questions about your friend?"

"Of course. Thanks so much for your help. I'm Ed Jaxson and my friend is Dora Creighton." He wiped sand off his forearms as he spoke.

"What happened this afternoon?"

Ed took a deep breath. "Dora and I have been dating for a couple of months. Since the weather's so nice, we decided to spend the day in Pine Cove. I know Dora's mentioned that she has asthma, but I've never seen her use an inhaler when we've been hiking or cycling. I don't think she even carries one with her."

I nodded, encouraging him to continue as I jotted down some notes. Saltwater from the zealous waves sprayed the air, and I took a few steps backward.

"We decided to wade in and cool off. We underestimated how rough the ocean is today. Before I knew what was happening, the waves pulled Dora out and under." Ed's voice briefly shook as he said, "I thought I'd lost her."

I patted Ed's shoulder. "It looks like Dora's conscious now. We're going to take her to the local hospital. The paramedics are on the way and will assess her in the back of our ambulance. They can decide if she needs advanced life support."

"Thank you. I don't know how I can repay everyone who saved Dora today. If it weren't for the people who pulled her out of the water, she wouldn't be here right now."

I nodded. "Yes, thank goodness there were people around to save her, and there were still lifeguards on duty in the next town over who could help. We're loading Dora into the ambulance now. Would you like to ride with us or meet us at the hospital?"

"I've got my car, so I'll meet you there," Ed said.

We parted ways, and I strode to the boardwalk to make sure the stretcher would be ready for Dora once the lifeguards carried her off the beach. I studied her face as they carefully placed her on the cot. It appeared an unnatural shade of white, matching the austere white blankets that covered the rest of her. Sand streaked her dark brown locks and left cheek. We rolled her to the back of the ambulance and loaded her inside. Paramedics Rose Anderson and William Moore were setting up their equipment.

Once I climbed into the ambulance, I introduced myself before switching Dora's oxygen from a portable unit to our main onboard tank. Rose passed me the blood-pressure cuff from their automatic unit so I could wrap it around Dora's right upper arm. "Her blood pressure is 140 over 86." I checked her radial pulse and counted her breathing rate. "Her pulse is 108 and her respirations are 32." A normal respiratory rate is between 12 and 20. Dora's elevated rate indicated she was still struggling to get enough air in despite the high-flow oxygen. "Her fingers are too cold to get a pulse ox reading." Despite the warm outdoor temperature, I cranked up the heat. I warmed up her fingers and rechecked her oxygen saturation level. "Her pulse ox is 98 percent on 15 liters per minute."

Rose placed her stethoscope on various parts of Dora's chest and upper back, carefully listening to her breath sounds. "Her lung sounds are diminished. I'm going to get the albuterol ready."

William attached Dora to a 12-lead EKG, confirming her elevated heart rate. "How are you feeling now?" he asked.

"I'm still having a hard time catching my breath, but I'm starting to feel a little better," Dora replied.

"Do you remember what happened today?" Rose asked.

Dora shuddered. "I remember the waves dragged me out, and then I felt my asthma kick in. I couldn't catch my breath. I got tired, and I couldn't swim anymore. I've never been so scared in my entire life. The last thing I remember is thinking I was going to die. I started praying, asking God to save me. Then it went dark until I woke up on the beach."

An answered prayer. I squeezed Dora's hand. "You're doing better now. We're on our way to the hospital."

As our ambulance worked its way along the oceanfront through

Marina Beach, I spotted another water rescue in progress. A Coast Guard boat was attempting to rescue two swimmers in distress.

William adjusted the flow rate of Dora's intravenous line. "It may not seem like it, but this is your lucky day. One of our patients drowned yesterday and two today."

Three lives lost due to rough surf in just two days. I reflected that life is tenuous. Dora could easily have become another statistic, just like the other three drowning victims. Instead, her desperate prayer and the heroic actions of fellow beachgoers saved her life. I was reminded of Isaiah 43:2: "When you pass through the waters, I will be with you."

We later learned that Dora went on to make a full recovery, and the two swimmers in distress in Marina Beach were successfully rescued by the Coast Guard in conjunction with a water rescue team that evening. In the span of just a few short weeks, I witnessed two miraculous water saves in our town: first Baby Eva and then Dora.

Two heavenly rescues and answered prayers.

About the Author

Andrea Jo Rodgers has been a volunteer EMT for more than 35 years and has responded to more than 9,500 first aid and fire calls. She holds a clinical doctorate in physical therapy and has worked as a physical therapist in a trauma center for 30 years.

MORE FIRST RESPONDER STORIES FROM HARVEST HOUSE PUBLISHERS

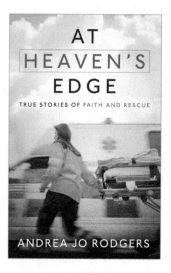

AT HEAVEN'S EDGE

TRUE STORIES OF FAITH AND RESCUE

ANDREA JO RODGERS

911…What Is Your Emergency?

Veteran EMT Andrea Rodgers has helped hundreds of people in their most vulnerable moments.

Some of the victims faced their mortality head-on and cried out to God for help. Many experienced fleeting but life-changing connections with their first responders. Often these crises became unexpected sources of inspiration.

Now Andrea shares brief, real-life stories of heroic courage in the face of fear. In times of intense suffering, she has repeatedly witnessed signs of God's quiet intervention and healing presence.

- A man is resuscitated after Andrea was able to repair a defibrillator—with her teeth!

- Several bystanders help rescue a young girl who is accidently buried alive in sand.

- Andrea also experienced some lighthearted moments, including the time she arrived at the scene of a crime only to find herself in the middle of a mystery dinner theater.

Experience the miracles and life-and-death drama as you look at life from heaven's edge.

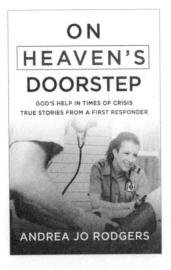

ON
HEAVEN'S
DOORSTEP

GOD'S HELP IN TIMES OF CRISIS
TRUE STORIES FROM A FIRST RESPONDER

ANDREA JO RODGERS

In Life or Death, There's Only One Guarantee— God Will Be There.

Medical emergencies are among life's most unexpected and terrifying realities. But isn't it reassuring in times of crisis that you can find hope and comfort in the hands of a loving God?

Encounter heart-stopping drama in these real-life stories of everyday people like you who found themselves on heaven's doorstep—fully dependent on the skilled and courageous efforts of first responders and on the mercy of God.

As you read these firsthand accounts of perilous situations with uncertain outcomes, you will experience a full spectrum of emotions, from tender heartache to tremendous joy. Through it all, you will witness God's amazing love and care for His children, both for those who are brought back from the edge and for those He welcomes into eternal fellowship with Him.

Be inspired as you go on call with veteran EMT Andrea Jo Rodgers and other brave professionals dedicated to helping when humanity is at its most frail.

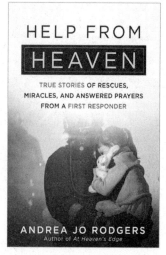

God, I Need You Now.

Experience the heart-pounding drama of real-life emergencies. Veteran EMT and physical therapist Andrea Jo Rodgers shares this all-new collection of accounts from her 30-plus years as a volunteer with her town's local first aid and emergency squad.

Arrive on the scene with Andrea and encounter…

- Lou, a dedicated war veteran who is granted a new tour of duty from God.

- A fearful flock of ducklings that slip down a storm drain during a false fire alarm.

- Everett, a resilient older man who goes for an unexpected ride on the hood of an intoxicated driver's car.

- Jenna, a young woman whose dangerous heart condition is both physical and emotional.

- Frank, a husband whose nasty fall down a flight of stairs earns him instant angel status from his devoted wife.

As you discover these and many more unforgettable stories, you'll be reminded that miracles do happen, whether it be through the heroic efforts of first responders, the Lord's divine intervention, or, often, both.

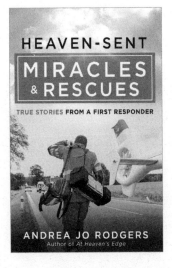

Do You Believe in Miracles?

For more than three decades Andrea Jo Rodgers has served her small-town community as a volunteer EMT. Over the years, the incredible events she's witnessed have taught her that behind the scenes of every dark and dire situation waits a God capable of doing the impossible to help, protect, and save those He loves.

In *Heaven-Sent Miracles and Rescues*, Andrea shares tales of amazing and supernatural occurrences she's seen from the frontline. From breathtaking water recoveries to heroic battles against housefires and astonishing interventions against medical crises, Andrea's accounts of emergency rescues will have you reading at the edge of your seat while reassuring you of God's awe-inspiring power over every circumstance.

Whether you're searching for affirmation that miracles still happen, or you simply love reading exciting and inspiring true stories, *Heaven-Sent Miracles and Rescues* will leave you uplifted, encouraged, and on the lookout for God's divine handiwork in your own day-to-day life.

Enjoy this excerpt from *Heaven-Sent Miracles and Rescues*
by Andrea Jo Rodgers

4

Surrounded by Love

My heart is glad and my tongue rejoices;
my body also will rest secure,
because you will not abandon me to the realm of the dead.

PSALM 16:9-10

N ow that we've had lunch, I think it's time for a shower," Arnie
Thompson suggested. He enjoyed working as a private duty aide
for Declan Walters in the Little River Assisted Living Facility. He'd
been taking care of Declan for the past six months and found him to
be the perfect mix of cooperative and feisty.

Arnie knew when he took the job that Declan wasn't in the best of
health. At 92 years young, he wasn't exactly what you'd call a "spring
chicken." The last few years had been rough. Declan had had a heart
attack the previous year and received an internal defibrillator. When
the two first met, Declan had just begun chemotherapy for brain cancer.

"You think I need a shower? Okay, you're the boss. As long as it's nice
and hot. You know how much I hate drafts," Declan said. Arnie walked
by Declan's side from the combination bedroom/living area down a
short hallway to the bathroom.

"Would you like to sit in the shower chair today?" Arnie asked.

"No, I prefer standing," Declan replied. He only used the shower
chair when he felt fatigued. His family had bought it when he began
chemotherapy treatments.

After about two minutes in the shower, Declan changed his mind. "On second thought, you can get me the chair. I'm starting to have trouble getting air in."

"I'll get your wheelchair, and we'll roll you out of here," Arnie said.

Declan's body grew limp. "I can't breathe."

Arnie grabbed Declan from behind and lowered him to the shower floor. "Call 911! I need help!" he yelled.

. . . .

DISPATCHER: "Request for first aid at the Little River Assisted Living Facility Room 12 for a 92-year-old male with difficulty breathing, currently in the shower and unable to get out."

I was driving toward a sporting goods store to take advantage of an after-Christmas sale when the call came. I lowered the speaker volume of my car radio so I could hear the dispatcher better. The Little River Assisted Living Facility was only a few blocks away in the opposite direction, so I did a U-turn and flipped on my blue emergency light.

As I pulled up to the facility, I noticed a Pine Cove patrol car was parked close by. I grabbed my first aid bag from my trunk. Fortunately, someone had propped open the front door. I ran inside and rushed along the hallway to Room 12.

When I entered, I found Officer Jack Endicott and a health aide lifting an unconscious man from the shower floor into a wheelchair.

"Andrea, if you roll the wheelchair out of here, Arnie and I will hold him and make sure he doesn't fall out," Officer Endicott said.

"Got it." I pulled the chair backward from the shower into the living room. I wasn't sure if our patient had a pulse or not. If he didn't, we'd have to start cardiopulmonary resuscitation (CPR) immediately.

"The patient's name is Declan Walters. This is his aide, Arnie. Declan began complaining of difficulty breathing and fell unconscious," Officer Endicott explained as we lifted him from the wheelchair onto the floor.

I knelt by Declan's head and slid my fingers onto his carotid artery. I detected a very faint pulse. However, he looked as though he could lose it at any moment. His face was stark white with a bluish undertone, and he didn't appear to be breathing adequately. "Let's use the bag valve mask." A bag valve mask (BVM) is used to provide positive-pressure ventilation to patients who are not breathing or who are not breathing adequately. A BVM can deliver up to 100 percent oxygen at 15 liters per minute with a reservoir bag.

Officer Endicott pulled the BVM out of his first aid bag. "I'll set it up."

Patsy, the competent and compassionate administrator of the facility, strode into the room. "Declan's a DNR." DNR stands for "do not resuscitate." In other words, if Declan went into cardiac arrest, we weren't allowed to do CPR.

Being a DNR changed our treatment plan. "Can we give him oxygen?" I asked.

"Yes, that would be fine. He has an oxygen machine at the far end of his bed. You can give him oxygen with a regular mask, but you can't assist his breathing with the BVM," Patsy said.

Declan's oxygen machine only provided up to six liters of oxygen via nasal cannula. Declan needed more than that. I placed a non-rebreather mask over his nose and mouth and adjusted the flow meter on our portable tank to 15 liters per minute.

"Let's lift him onto the bed," Officer Endicott suggested. "Since we can't do CPR, we can at least make him more comfortable." The four of us lifted him as a team, careful to support his head as we laid him on the bed.

Within seconds, Declan's eyes fluttered open. He struggled to sit up. "I need my clothes on!" he exclaimed.

A wave of relief washed over me. It appeared Declan was going to be okay after all. Rosy pink stained his cheeks, a welcome change from his earlier pallor.

Arnie raised the head of the bed and began dressing Declan. "You gave me a scare," he chided.

I fished a pulse oximeter out of my first aid bag. I placed the device on Declan's right index finger to determine his oxygen level, but I couldn't get a reading. I tried a different finger. No luck.

"Here, try mine," Officer Endicott suggested as he passed me an oximeter from his first aid kit. I slipped it on Declan's index finger. His reading was 80 percent. Dangerously low.

I placed a blood-pressure cuff around Declan's upper arm. Unfortunately, after I pumped up the cuff and listened for Declan's pressure, I couldn't hear anything. *Not a good sign.*

I placed my index and middle fingers along the thumb side of Declan's wrist to check his pulse. "It's 59," I told Officer Endicott, who jotted it down on his notepad.

I patted Declan's shoulder. "As soon as the ambulance arrives, we'll take you to the hospital."

"You can't. He's on hospice," Patsy said. "I'll call the hospice nurse right away."

Normally, we aren't dispatched for hospice patients—those who are terminally ill and are receiving palliative comfort care. Emergency calls go to a hospice nurse rather than EMS (emergency medical services). Apparently, we had only ended up here this afternoon because of the extraordinary circumstances surrounding Declan's collapse in the shower. The news that Declan was on hospice further complicated matters.

Declan's breathing turned fast and shallow. His eyes grew wide, and he grasped Arnie's forearm.

Patsy stepped out of the room to call hospice and returned a few minutes later. "The hospice nurse is at least forty-five minutes away, maybe more. She said she's on her way here and doesn't want you to take Declan to the hospital. I realize you don't have to stay, but we don't have oxygen tanks here."

I squeezed Declan's hand. "We're going to stay." Perhaps we were there by accident, but we would stay. Volunteer first responders don't leave when someone needs them. It would be acting against our genetic makeup.

Declan's room had a sliding glass door that exited directly outdoors. I watched as Jose Sanchez parked our ambulance alongside the room, rather than in front of the facility. The rest of the volunteer EMS squad, including Ted O'Malley, Mason Chapman, Greg Turner, Meg Potter, and Sadie Martinez, soon stepped into the room. I explained to them Declan's condition.

Meg squeezed between the bedrail and wall on the far side of the bed. "I'll try once more to get a blood pressure reading." Still no luck.

Declan's anxiety increased, and he grew restless.

Ted, Mason, Greg, Meg, Sadie, Arnie, and I formed a human circle around Declan's bed. Sadie gently stroked his foot. Arnie patted his shoulder, while I stroked Declan's head.

A few minutes later, paramedics Arthur Williamson and Kennisha Smythe arrived from the hospital. Paramedics, who provide advanced life support (ALS), are paid employees of the hospital. Arthur and Kennisha, who have been partners for several years, are both experienced and knowledgeable.

"Technically, since he's a DNR on hospice, we really can't get involved," Arthur explained. "You need the hospice nurse."

Patsy frowned. "We're not sure when she's going to get here. She's at least forty-five minutes out. Do you have any suggestions?"

"Why don't you ask the hospice nurse if you can give him an Ativan?" Arthur asked. Ativan is a medication used to treat anxiety.

"Okay, I'll call her back and get an order to administer that." Pasty hurried out of the room to place the phone call.

Our squad members provided comforting words and touch to Declan until Patsy returned with an Ativan pill in her hand. "There's still no exact ETA on when the hospice nurse will arrive. I also spoke to Declan's family to let them know what's going on. His son lives in Virginia, and his daughter is in Maine. Fortunately, they just saw him a few days ago for Christmas."

"I'm afraid it's too late for Ativan," Kennisha said. "Declan's no longer alert enough to swallow a pill. Do you have it in an injectable form?"

Patsy shook her head. "I'll call the hospice nurse back."

"Do you have a hospice package here?" I asked. "Maybe something in the minifridge?" I knew from experience that patients on hospice often have a special kit in the refrigerator that includes medications such as morphine.

We searched Declan's fridge and room, but to no avail. At this point, 25 minutes had passed since we'd first arrived. Greg switched the portable oxygen tank to a fresh one.

"Let me try to get another set of vitals," Meg said. She placed the pulse oximeter on Declan's finger. "His pulse is 70, but his pulse ox is only 66 percent, even with the high-flow oxygen."

Arthur's radio crackled. "I'm sorry, but we have to leave now. We have another assignment."

"Thanks for your help," I murmured. I was grateful for their input. Now, we were on our own.

Declan's pulse ox reading no longer registered. His gaze became unseeing. He closed his eyes. His breathing rate slowed. He began slipping away.

"Your family called," I told him. "They're so happy they saw you at Christmas. They're sending all their love." I gently stroked the top of Declan's head as I spoke. Although he was now unconscious, I hoped he heard what I was saying.

Patsy rejoined us. "I'm sorry to say there's still no arrival time for hospice. I'm working on finding out if there's something else we can do for him until the nurse gets here."

"I don't think she's going to make it on time. He's going to pass soon," I said.

"Oh no! Poor Declan." Patsy blinked back tears. I could tell she cared greatly for him. "I'm going to call his family again. I told them he wasn't feeling well but not that he might expire. I'll call back the hospice nurse too." She stroked Declan's arm before leaving the room.

Declan's complexion turned gray. His breathing switched to agonal respirations, which are ineffective, gasping breaths.

We took turns speaking soothingly to Declan. Since his loved ones lived many miles away, we became his surrogate family. We poured love on Declan like syrup on a buttermilk pancake. There wasn't an inch of him that wasn't covered. We engulfed him with a giant blanket of human love.

Declan took his last breath and transitioned peacefully from his earthly life to his eternal life with Christ.

I think most of us contemplate at some point or another what our ending will be like. Will we be young? Old? Alone? With family? Will we be staring at the pearly gates of heaven? Have we accepted Christ as our Savior?

On that day, Jesus granted us the opportunity to assist in a way first responders normally don't. We're usually in the business of saving lives rather than providing a loving send-off.

Despite the sadness of the situation, I felt privileged to be with Declan in his final hour on earth. And I felt blessed to witness an amazing display of kindness, patience, and love from my fellow squad members and the staff at Little River Assisted Living Facility.

To learn more about Harvest House books and
to read sample chapters, visit our website:

www.HarvestHousePublishers.com

HARVEST HOUSE PUBLISHERS
EUGENE, OREGON